Presented to

_____

From

_____

Date

_____

The Baker

Bible

Handbook

For Kids

Baker Bible Handbook for Kids

Copyright © 1998 Educational Publishing Concepts, Inc., Wheaton, IL

Produced with the assistance of The Livingstone Corporation.
Terry Jean Day, Daryl J. Lucas, Collette Placek, Carol J. Smith, project staff.

Scripture quotations are taken from the Holy Bible, New Living Translation, copyright © 1996. Used by permission of Tyndale House Publishers, Inc., Wheaton, Illinois 60189. All rights reserved.

Published in Grand Rapids, Michigan by Baker Book House.

ISBN 0-8010-4409-X

Printed in the United States of America.

1 2 3 4 5 6 7 8 9 — 0 2 01 00 99 98

The Baker

Bible

Handbook
For Kids

Terry Jean Day
Carol J. Smith

Contributing Editor
Daryl J. Lucas

Published in
association

BAKER
A DIVISION OF
Baker Book House Co

Contents

The New Testament

How to Use the *Baker Bible Handbook for Kids*

A long, long time ago, in a land very far away, a man took up a pen. He sat down and looked at a blank piece of paper. And he began to write, "In the beginning, God created the heavens and the earth." And he wrote, and wrote, and wrote. His name was Moses.

Moses gave us the first five books of the Bible, Genesis through Deuteronomy. But his books were not the only books to be written. It would take 61 more books, at least 36 other writers, and about 1,500 years to finish the job. Only after John wrote the last letter in Revelation was the Bible complete.

And that makes the Bible a lot like salad—a little of this, a little of that, all mixed in together. If you have ever flipped through the pages of a Bible, you know that it is a big, complicated, unusual book. It has all kinds of writing. It has very long and very short parts. It has a lot of pages. It needs a handbook.

Bird's eye view

This book has one purpose: To help you get a handle on the Bible. Think of being in an airplane high up above the ground. When you look out the window, you can see the lay of the land. You are up above all the detail, where you can see the big picture. Up in the plane, you can see everything at once.

That is what this book does for you. It tells you about the big ideas in the Bible. It tells you about the main people. It gives the main points of every Bible book. It helps you see how all of it is put together.

What's in here?

The Baker Bible Handbook for Kids has two parts:
(1) Information about the individual books of the Bible (Overviews), and
(2) Information about the whole Bible all together. Here's the breakdown:

Overview Overall

The Overviews are the heart of the book. (If you count the pages, you will notice that it takes up the most space.) They will give you the headlines on each and every Bible book. If you need to get up to speed on this or that book of the Bible, check out the Overviews.

To learn about the Bible as a whole, check out Part 2. In fact, we suggest that you just start reading it. You will soon get a grasp of everything there is to know about the Bible.

That's it! The Baker Bible Handbook for Kids is here for you. Consider it your personal jet, all fueled up and ready to take you up high, where you can get some perspective. May God bless you as you study his Word.

Terry Jean Day, Carol J. Smith, Daryl J. Lucas

THE OLD TESTAMENT

GENESIS

WHY THIS BOOK?

Genesis is "the Book of Beginnings." It doesn't just go way back, it goes all the way back. It starts at the beginning of all beginnings. It starts at creation. It introduces us to the universe, to Earth, to people. It introduces us to sin and to God's plans for the world. It explains what everything is and how it all got started.

Genesis also introduces us to the nation of Israel. This is very important because Israel takes the spotlight in the Old Testament. God chose Israel to be his very own people. They play a part in every bit of God's efforts to save us from sin and win us to himself. We can't understand the Bible without knowing about these people. Genesis lets us meet them for the first time.

By introducing us to all of that, Genesis introduces us to God. We learn who God is and what he really wants from us. It is an amazing bit of history from start to finish.

OUTLINE

A. Creation (1:1–2:3)
God creates the universe and everything in it. He makes people in his own image.

B. Adam and Eve (2:4–5:32)
Adam and Eve have all they need. But the serpent gets them to disobey God anyway. That brings sin into the world. Cain kills his brother.

C. Noah, the flood, and the tower of Babel (6:1–11:32)

The world gets so bad that God floods the whole earth. Only Noah and those on the boat with him survive.

D. Abraham and Sarah *(12:1–25:18)*

God chooses Abraham and Sarah to be the ancestors of his own people. God promises to bless the whole earth through this new people of God.

E. Isaac and Rebekah *(25:19–28:9)*

The first generation of Abraham's descendants settle in Canaan, the land of God's promise. God renews his promise to Isaac.

F. The story of Jacob and Esau *(28:10–36:43)*

Jacob leaves home, and God promises to take care of him and to bless him just as he did Abraham and Isaac.

G. The story of Joseph *(37:1–50:26)*

Joseph's brothers sell him into slavery in Egypt. But God watches over him and soon Joseph is ruler of all Egypt under Pharaoh. Through Joseph, God saves his people from famine as Jacob's whole family moves to Egypt.

FAQs

Q: Is Genesis really true?

A: Yes, we know it is true because it is part of God's Word.

Jesus quoted from Genesis a few times. He referred to Noah, for example.

Q: Why did God ask Adam where he was and if he had eaten the fruit he wasn't supposed to eat? Didn't God know?

A: God knows everything, but he wanted Adam to admit what he had done and to repent.

Q: Why didn't Noah take more people into the boat with his family?

A: The Bible says, "Noah warned the world of God's righteous judgment" (2 Peter 2:5), but it seems that people did not believe him.

LOOKOUT FOR . . .

As you read through Genesis, be on the lookout for . . .

God's messages to people. God speaks and appears to people several times at this important time of history. Take note of what he says.

Abraham. He's a main, very important person in the stories of Genesis. God chooses to bless the whole world through him. His name comes up again and again in the Bible.

Promises to Abraham. They set the stage for a lot of what happens in the rest of the Bible.

Joseph. He plays a big part in his family's travels. And what he does sets the stage for Exodus.

SPECIAL REPORT

Covenant. A covenant is a pact or agreement of loyalty between two people. Genesis records two covenants that God made with people. The first was with Noah. God promised not to destroy the earth by flood ever again *(9:8-17)*. The rainbow became a sign of this covenant, which is still at work today.

God also made a very important covenant with Abram. God promised to bless Abram by making him the father of a great nation *(12:1 3; 15:18-21)*. God would give land to this nation and bless the entire world through its people. God renewed, or restated, this promise to Abraham's son Isaac *(26:2-5)* and to his grandson Jacob *(28:13-15)*.

STUDY QUESTIONS

• How did people become rulers of the earth? *(Genesis 1:26-28)*
• Why did Adam and Eve have to leave the garden of Eden? *(Genesis 3:22-23)*
• How did Noah and his family get the animals to go into the boat? *(Genesis 6:20)*
• Why did Abram leave home and go to Canaan? *(Genesis 12:1-3)*
• Why did God allow Joseph to suffer? *(Genesis 50:20)*

Exodus

WHY THIS BOOK?

After 400 years in Egypt, the Israelites were finally leaving! God knew about all their misery as slaves. It was time to move out. He was taking them to the land he had promised to Abraham.

"Exodus" means "departure" or "leaving." This book tells how God freed the Israelites from slavery in Egypt. Pharaoh didn't want to lose his slave labor. God used ten plagues to convince Pharaoh to let the Israelites leave. Pharaoh must have had a hard head as well as a hard heart! God protected his people from the plagues. He also saved the Israelites from drowning in the Red Sea.

The people had a lot to learn about being God's special people. For example, they did not always trust that God would provide food and water. They also made an idol and worshiped it. But God loved them anyway.

VITAL STATS/OUTLINE

A. Israel becomes a nation *(1–4)*

The family of Jacob has grown to be a whole nation. Moses is born and adopted by Pharaoh's daughter. He grows up and is called by God to rescue the Hebrews from Egypt *(3:1-22)*.

B. Beginning of the rescue

(5–11)

Moses returns to Egypt to convince Pharaoh to free the Hebrews. God sends ten plagues to help Pharaoh make up his mind.

C. The Passover and Exodus *(12–15)*

The angel of death comes. The Passover begins. The people leave Egypt. God parts the Red Sea.

D. Wilderness travels *(16–19)*

The Hebrews grow weary and start to complain even though God is providing for them in every way.

E. Mount Sinai *(20–23)*

God gives Moses the Ten Commandments. God instructs his people.

F. The Tabernacle *(24–40)*

Moses and the elders meet with God. The people make a golden calf. Moses breaks the Ten Commandments tablets so they have to be written down again. The Tabernacle is prepared.

FAQs

Q: Why did Pharaoh like Joseph and his family but make slaves of the Israelites?

A: The Pharaoh who knew Joseph was different from the Pharaoh who enslaved the Israelites. Four hundred years had passed. During that time, the Israelites had gotten very numerous. This Pharaoh feared they would fight against him.

Q: Why did God send plagues on Egypt?

A: Egyptians worshiped many false gods. The Lord showed his power against these false deities with each one of the plagues.

Q: Why did the Israelites complain after they left Egypt?

A: The Israelites missed the Egyptian food and were afraid they wouldn't have water.

Q: What were the Israelites doing while God was giving the Ten Commandments to Moses?

A: They became impatient for Moses to return and made a golden calf as an idol and worshiped it.

LOOKOUT FOR . . .

As you read through Exodus, be on the lookout for . . .

Distrust. The people fail to trust God over and over again, even though he takes care of them.

Signs. God gives the Hebrews many signs to help them believe.

Miracles. Throughout Exodus God works many miracles and wonders.

SPECIAL REPORT

Plague. A plague is something so bad and so big that it affects everyone around it. God used ten different plagues to convince Pharaoh to let the Israelites go. Small groups of locusts, frogs, and flies can occur in nature. But when swarms of them appear all at once, then it is called a plague. Egypt had more than just a few thousand flies. It had millions of flies everywhere! God used these 10 plagues to show his power to Pharaoh. Still, Pharaoh did not listen.

STUDY QUESTIONS

• What instructions did Pharaoh give the Hebrew midwives? *(Exodus 1:15-16)*

• What did the midwives do? *(Exodus 1:17-21)*

• How did Moses' mother obey Pharaoh—but not quite? *(Exodus 1:22–2:4)*

• How did God get Moses' attention? *(Exodus 3:1-6)*

• How did blood save the Israelites? *(Exodus 12:21-30)*

• How did God lead the Israelites out of Egypt? *(Exodus 13:20-22)*

• In what ways did God fight against the Egyptians as they chased the Israelites? *(Exodus 14:21-31)*

• What were some of the laws of justice and mercy that God gave to the Israelites? *(Exodus 23:1-9)*

LEVITICUS

WHY THIS BOOK?

Making the Israelites into a special nation took a lot of work. God had to teach his people a whole new way of life. So he gave them a lot of instructions on how to live and worship. It is called the book of Leviticus.

Leviticus was a handbook for the Hebrew priests. It teaches about the sacrifices that God wanted people to offer for forgiveness. It is also a guide for holy living. Leviticus mentions holiness dozens of times. A special verse says, "You must be holy because I, the Lord your God, am holy" (*Leviticus 19:2*).

God gave specific directions for worshiping him. Two of Aaron's sons disobeyed God's rules for worship. It was such a serious matter that they actually died. The offerings described in Leviticus help us understand why Jesus Christ came and died. These laws were fulfilled when Jesus died on the cross.

VITAL STATS/OUTLINE

A. The system of sacrifices and the priesthood *(1–10)*
Notes on how to offer sacrifices. The priests begin their ministry.

B. Laws of sanitation and health *(11–15)*

Notes on how to keep themselves and their camp clean and healthy.

C. The annual atonement and its observance *(16–17)*

Notes on how to celebrate the Day of Atonement. This includes the scapegoat.

D. Holy living *(18–22)*

Notes on actions that God hates. Also many civil and moral laws appear here.

E. The priesthood, its services, and duties *(23–24)*

Notes on the festivals and special days called holy days (like our "holidays") and the role of the priests in the celebrations.

F. Special years; warning and blessing; vows and tithes *(25–27)*

Notes on traditions the people should keep such as the Sabbath year and the Year of Jubilee. Also, the assurance that there will be blessings for obedience and punishments for disobedience.

FAQs

Q: Why did the people have to sacrifice animals?

A: God wanted the people to understand how serious sin is.

Q: What kinds of animals did God want for offerings?

A: The offerings that God required were bulls, lambs, goats, doves, and pigeons, depending on the occasion. But always the offering had to be a perfect animal. It had to be the best—not anything that had a blemish or disease.

Q: Why did the people have to keep on offering sacrifices?

A: These sacrifices did not really take away sin, but they did make amends for the offense against God. People sin again and again, so before Jesus came, people had to offer sacrifices again and again. Jesus' death on the cross did take away sin; his sacrifice for sin needed to be done only once.

LOOKOUT FOR . . .

As you read through Leviticus, be on the lookout for . . .

Holiness. This whole book is about holiness. Over and over God teaches the people to be holy.

Priests. This book is like a how-to manual for priests. Because of this you will see a lot of references to priests.

Sacrifices. Sacrifices are to be an important part of Jewish worship. The first part of Leviticus tells exactly how these sacrifices are to be done.

Festivals and holy days. God uses the festivals and holy days of the Jews to remind them of the miracles he has performed among them, just as Christmas reminds us of Jesus' birth.

SPECIAL REPORT

Passover lamb. The Passover was the last plague on Egypt. The oldest son of each household died unless the blood of a lamb was smeared on the frame of the front door of the house. The Israelites continued to celebrate this Passover by having a special meal each year at the same time.

This meal reminded them of God's rescue. But it also taught them about the work that Christ would one day do. When Jesus died on the cross, he became our Passover lamb and saved us from death (John 1:29,36).

STUDY QUESTIONS

• How did Aaron and the priests know that God cared about holiness? (Leviticus 10:1-11)

• What rewards did God promise to the Israelites if they obeyed him? (Leviticus 26:1-13)

• What did God say to the people who did not want to obey him? (Leviticus 26:14-16)

• How do we know that the book of Leviticus is important? (Leviticus 27:34)

NUMBERS

WHY THIS BOOK?

After all the Lord did in Egypt to prove he is God, the people of Israel still doubted him. The book of Numbers tells about the test of faith they faced.

The book gets its name from the way the people of Israel were numbered, or counted, twice. The first time they were counted was soon after they left Egypt. God wanted Moses to know how many fighting men he had to go into battle. But the people grumbled and complained and did not believe God could take them into the Promised Land.

Moses sent 12 spies to see how they should conquer the land. When they returned, ten said it was impossible. Only two— Joshua and  Caleb—said, yes there were giants, yes it was a big job, but yes, the Lord would give them the victory as he had said. But the people listened to the men who were afraid. They refused to go into battle.

Because they doubted, they spent 40 years wandering in the desert. None of those who doubted God lived to see his promise fulfilled.

At the end of that long, winding trip, Moses counted the people again.

VITAL STATS/OUTLINE

A. Numbering and organizing the people *(1–5)*
Israel does its first census and then begins to assign chores to certain clans.

B. Preparation for the journey *(6–10)*
The people get ready to travel by offering sacrifices and celebrating their first Passover in freedom.

C. March to Kadesh Barnea *(11–12)*
The people complain because the trip is so difficult. Some of them even wish they were back in Egypt. God provides for them by sending quail for them to eat.

D. The twelve spies *(13–14)*
Scouts explore the land. Only two bring back a good report. The other ten are afraid that the Israelites will never be able to conquer the land. The people become very upset and afraid. Once again, they fail to trust God.

E. Repeated lack of faith *(15–21)*
The people rebel against Moses and God uses an earthquake to punish them. Aaron's family begins to serve as priests when a walking stick

begins to bud as if it were a plant in the ground.

F. Balaam's prophecy and a problem with Moab (22–25)

Balaam comes to curse Israel, but blesses it instead. His very own donkey talks to him. Then the Israelites get duped by idol worshipers.

G. Another census, regulations, and events (26–36)

The second census is taken. Joshua becomes the next leader. Two of the tribes receive their land because they want to settle before crossing the Jordan River.

FAQs

Q: Why were the people counted?

A: The men who were 20 years or older were counted to serve in the army.

Q: Since there were no phones, how did Moses let the people know when they were moving?

A: God told Moses to make two silver trumpets to use for calling the people together and moving the camp.

Q: Why were Miriam and Aaron jealous of their brother, Moses?

A: They wanted to be important leaders too.

Q: Why didn't the spies want to enter Canaan?

A: The spies saw good land and plenty of food. But the people of Canaan were so large that the spies felt like grasshoppers and were afraid.

Q: Why couldn't Balaam curse the Israelites like Balak wanted him to?

A: Balaam tried three times to curse the Israelites, but God would not let him. Every time Balaam tried to curse them, a blessing came out of his mouth.

LOOKOUT FOR . . .

As you read through Numbers, be on the lookout for . . .

Rules and regulations. Numbers gives many "how-to's," especially to priests.

Lack of faith The people of God keep losing their faith even though God has provided for them.

Counting. Two times the whole Hebrew nation is counted. They have no computers or adding machines, so this is a big job.

SPECIAL REPORT

Census. A census is a count of people. We still take censuses today to know how many people live in our cities and towns. It is a big job for us even though we have phones and computers and adding machines.

Numbers

The nation of Israel was a baby nation that had never taken a census of themselves before. They had started with Joseph and his brothers. These men had families, then their families had families, and a nation was born. It was a big job, then, when they got out into the desert and decided to count just how many people they had with them. The number was over 600,000. That number is bigger than many modern towns!

At the end of Numbers the Israelites took another census. Both of these censuses helped the people organize into family groups. They also helped Moses assign land so that the families would have somewhere to settle in their new home.

STUDY QUESTIONS

• How did God guide the people from place to place? *(Numbers 9:15-23)*

• What was manna like? *(Numbers 11:7-9)*

• How did Moses lose his opportunity to enter the Promised Land? *(Numbers 20:2-12)*

• How did Balaam's donkey make a fool out of Balaam when he tried to curse God's people? *(Numbers 22:21-33)*

• Before he died, what did Moses ask God to do? *(Numbers 27:12-23)*

• What was a city of refuge? *(Numbers 35:9-15)*

DEUTERONOMY

WHY THIS BOOK?

Deuteronomy is a book of memories, like a scrapbook. Moses had spent 40 years taking the Israelites on a journey that was supposed to have taken only two years. The people who disobeyed God had all died without seeing the Promised Land. But now the people who came after them were about to enter Canaan. They were ready to go.

So Moses reminded them of all the Lord had done for them over the past 40 years. He repeated the law for them. He encouraged them to believe and obey God and do God's will.

Moses reminded the people of God's promises for obedience and the punishment for disobedience. He also blessed the people. Then Moses made Joshua their new leader.

Deuteronomy is the fifth book of law. It is a book that Jesus knew well. It is the book that Jesus quoted when Satan was trying to tempt him to disobey the Father.

VITAL STATS/OUTLINE

A. History of the journey (1–5)

The Hebrews leave Mount Sinai where they received the Ten Commandments. Moses appoints leaders of each tribe. They wander

31

through the desert and fight several battles.

B. Rules and regulations (5–26)

Moses reviews the Ten Commandments and many other rules for living.

C. Curses and blessings (27–30)

Moses reminds the people that they will receive blessings for obedience and curses for disobedience.

D. Moses' successor (31–34)

Joshua becomes the national leader and Moses says good-bye to his people. Moses never gets to enter the Promised Land.

FAQs

Q: Why wasn't Moses allowed to enter the Promised Land?

A: Moses disobeyed God. Moses was angry at the people for complaining. Instead of speaking to the rock for water to come, as God had told him to, Moses hit the rock two times (because he was angry).

Q: Why was Moses afraid the people would forget God?

A: Moses knew that when the people had plenty of food and an easy life they might forget to trust God.

Q: How did God take care of his people in the desert?

A: God sent manna for them to eat and water for them to drink. Also, their sandals did not wear out for 40 years!

LOOKOUT FOR . . .

As you read through Deuteronomy, be on the lookout for . . .

The Ten Commandments. This book retells some of the stories from Exodus, including the Ten Commandments.

God's faithfulness. Even when the Hebrews do not have much faith, God faithfully takes care of them.

God's requirements. God is very clear with the people what he wants: their worship, love, and obedience.

Celebrations. God does not just give his people rules to follow, he also tells them to hold festivals that remind them of the good things God has done.

SPECIAL REPORT

The Promised Land. Many years before the Exodus from Egypt, God had promised Abraham some land. That land was what we know today as Israel. It is where you will find the Jordan River, the Dead Sea, and the town of Bethlehem. You may hear of people who go to "the Holy Land." When they say this they mean the land where Jesus grew up. It is the same land that God promised Abraham and the same land that the Hebrews traveled to from Egypt.

You may also hear of fighting in Israel today. That is because many years after Jesus lived there, the Israelites were made to leave again. When they came back to claim their land (as they did in Deuteronomy) it had been settled by other people and was called by a different name.

Deuteronomy describes the time just before the nation first entered the Promised Land. They are just across the river from this land. Moses even goes to the top of the hill to look over and see the land that is theirs. This land has always been and always will be important to the Jewish people.

STUDY QUESTIONS

• What are the Ten Commandments? *(Deuteronomy 5:6-21)*

• What is one reason God wants people to obey him with their whole heart? *(Deuteronomy 5:29)*

• How did God say parents should teach their children God's commandments? *(Deuteronomy 6:6-9)*

• Before Moses died, what was so important about the advice he gave Joshua? *(Deuteronomy 31:7-8)*

• What was Moses like at the end of his life? *(Deuteronomy 34:7)*

• How was Moses special? *(Deuteronomy 34:10-12)*

JOSHUA

WHY THIS BOOK?

It took a strong leader to take the Israelites into the Promised Land. After Moses died, Joshua took up where Moses left off. The people finally were ready to follow God's plan. It may seem like a strange plan, but it worked. The book of Joshua tells about the battles and experiences the Israelites had in taking the land that God had given them.

God dried up the Jordan River so the Israelites could cross on dry land. Marching around a city doesn't sound like the way to win a battle. But this time the Israelites obeyed. Once every day for six days they marched around Jericho. On the seventh day, they marched around seven times. On the seventh time, Joshua told the people to shout. They shouted and the walls of Jericho came crashing down.

This was just the beginning of conquering the land God had promised to Abraham, Isaac, and Jacob. Sometimes the people still disobeyed and then they failed. But God took them into Canaan and gave each tribe a new home.

Joshua's instructions to the people are also in this book.

Joshua

Like Moses, Joshua wanted his people to obey God and enjoy God's blessings.

VITAL STATS/OUTLINE

A. Joshua becomes the leader *(1)*

God tells Joshua how to be successful. Joshua takes charge of the people and begins to lead them.

B. Taking over Canaan *(2–12)*

Some spies go to Jericho and are taken care of by a woman named Rahab. God parts the Jordan River for all the people to cross. The people circle Jericho and the walls fall down, except for Rahab's house. Achan gets greedy and everyone suffers for it.

C. Dividing and settling the land *(13–22)*

The people settle the land and continue to fight the few people who will not let them settle in peace.

D. Joshua says good-bye *(23–24)*

Joshua gives a final, inspiring speech. He reminds the people of all that God has done for them.

FAQs

Q: What made Joshua brave enough to take Moses' place?

A: God told Joshua that he would be with him wherever he went.

Q: Why did Rahab hide the Israelite spies from her own people?

A: Rahab had heard about God's power, and she decided to follow him instead of the false gods that her people worshiped.

Q: How did the Israelite soldiers know which people were on their side?

A: Rahab put a red cord in the window of her house. All of her family in the house were saved from death in the battle.

Q: How come the Israelites could defeat great Jericho so easily but were defeated by the small town of Ai?

A: Achan had hidden some treasures in his tent against God's instructions. All the Israelites suffered for his selfishness by losing the battle with Ai.

LOOKOUT FOR . . .

As you read through Joshua, be on the lookout for . . .

Battles. There are many important and miraculous battles fought during this time.

Good leadership. Joshua is a strong leader and he takes good care of God's people.

Wins and losses. Notice that when the people obey and trust God, the battles go well. But when they do not . . . watch what happens.

Miracles. God keeps doing miracles for his people. The sun stands still, the waters part, and many other miracles take place.

SPECIAL REPORT

Tribes. Any time the land is divided in the Old Testament "tribes" will usually be mentioned. Tribes are very large family units—not just the parents and the kids, but all their extended relatives too. A tribe starts way back with the parents' parents and the grandparents' parents. A tribe traces its roots way back to one person; the whole tribe is descended from that person (children of his children and their children and their children and so on).

The tribes of Israel come from Jacob's twelve sons and two of his grandsons. (Jacob was Abraham's grandson. God promised Abraham that his descendants would be as many as the stars in the sky.) Whenever the book of Joshua talks about a tribe, it means the families that came from one of those sons. Every tribe got some land except the tribe of Levi. Levi is the tribe that Moses and his family came from. That tribe became priests, leaders of worship, and caretakers of the Temple. Because they worked in the Temple, they did not need land at that time.

STUDY QUESTIONS

• What made Rahab want to help the Israelite spies? (Joshua 2:8-13)

• Why did Joshua set up 12 stones at Gilgal? (Joshua 4:19-24)

• How did Joshua make sure the people knew what God expected and what he promised? (Joshua 8:30-35)

• How did the Gibeonites trick Joshua? (Joshua 9:1-27)

• How did Joshua gain extra daylight hours to win a battle? (Joshua 10:9-14)

• How did the Lord fulfill his promises to the Israelites? (Joshua 21:43-45)

JUDGES

WHY THIS BOOK?

The great leaders Moses and Joshua were dead. The Israelites had seen God keep his promise to take them into the Promised Land. But they became lazy about obeying the Lord's commands. They failed to remove the sinful people who lived in Canaan. Instead, the Israelites learned the ways of their enemies. The book of Judges tells of the sin and sorrow the Israelites went through.

The people of Israel married people who worshiped idols. Soon the Israelites themselves were worshiping false gods. The  Lord punished them for turning their backs on him. Instead of enjoying the good things of the Promised Land, the Israelites suffered war, slavery, and hardship. But then they cried to God for help, and he sent a judge to lead them in battle and bring them back to himself.

But again and again, the Israelites forgot their promise to obey the Lord. So, again and again, God would allow their enemies to dcfeat them. Then the Israelites would be sorry for their sins and ask him to save them, and God would send another judge to help them.

For about 325 years this pattern continued. God used 12 men and women to judge and help his people. The judges were not perfect people, but they submitted to God's leadership. He used them, in return, to help his people.

VITAL STATS/OUTLINE

A. Introduction *(1–2)*

The Hebrews do not conquer all of the Promised Land. That means some of their enemies are left there to cause trouble. These enemies are who the Judges have to fight.

B. Israel's first judges *(3)*

Othniel, then Ehud, and then Shamgar serve as Israel's judges.

C. Sisera's defeat *(4–5)*

Deborah judges Israel with Barak's help.

E. Gideon judges Israel *(6–10)*

Gideon, then Abimelech, then Tola, then Jair serve as judges.

E. Jephthah judges Israel *(11–12)*

Jephthah, then Ibzan, then Elon, then Abdon serve as judges.

F. Samson *(13–16)*

Samson learns his lessons the hard way through mistakes and failures.

G. Israel is without a leader *(17–21)*

This is a time of much confusion and sin in the life of God's people.

FAQs

Q: How come God didn't keep his promise to help his people?

A: God promised to bless the Israelites if they obeyed him. When they disobeyed him, he stopped helping them. But he still kept his promise to bless all the nations through Israel (by sending the Savior).

Q: What were judges?

A: Judges were leaders whom God called to help the Israelites. They would show the people their sin, encourage them, lead them in battle, and draw them back to the Lord. Sometimes they ruled over the people foolishly.

Q: Who were the greatest judges?

A: Most people think of Gideon, Deborah, and Samson as the greatest judges.

LOOKOUT FOR . . .

As you read through Judges, be on the lookout for . . .

Falling away. Israel goes through cycles of following God, then falling away from God.

Revival. Good strong judges help bring Israel back around.

Rebellion and sin. Whenever the Israelites fall away from God, they lead evil and violent lives.

SPECIAL REPORT

Nazirites. Nazirites were people who kept very strict religious laws. A person could be a Nazirite for his or her whole life or for only a short time.

Nazirites did not drink any wine or eat grapes. This showed that they were willing to give up something enjoyable for wholehearted service to God. They never used a razor. This showed personal strength and vitality. People who stopped being Nazirites burned their hair as a sacrifice to the Lord. Also, the Nazirites could not touch or be near any dead body (see Numbers 6:6).

There are three men we know of who were Nazirites for life: Samson, Samuel, and John the Baptist.

STUDY QUESTIONS

• Why did Othniel become the first judge of Israel?
(Judges 3:7-11)

• What went wrong with Israel during the time of the judges?
(Judges 21:25)

RUTH

WHY THIS BOOK?

It was a dark time in the history of the Israelites. Everyone was doing what he or she wanted. Very few people were trying to obey the Lord. Not many people thought of helping others. Right in the middle of this unhappy time of the judges, there were three people whose lives were different. Their story is told in the book of Ruth.

Naomi, Ruth, and Boaz did not just think of themselves. They thought about what would be good for others and helped others in need. They also loved God.

Ruth was a widow (that means her husband had died). She lived in Moab with her mother-in-law, Naomi. Naomi was a widow, too. Naomi wanted to return to Bethlehem in Judah. She told Ruth to stay in Moab and go back to her people. But Ruth loved her mother-in-law very much. Ruth promised to go with Naomi and take care of her. Ruth wanted to worship the true God also.

When Naomi and Ruth arrived in Bethlehem, Ruth worked to get food for them. Boaz was kind and told Ruth to work in his fields and stay close to his workers. In the end, Boaz married Ruth. Then he and Ruth took care of Naomi

together.

The book of Ruth shows that no matter how bad things are, there are always some people who love and obey God.

VITAL STATS/OUTLINE

A. Naomi in Moab (1)

Naomi's husband and sons die, and she decides to move back to Bethlehem. One of her daughters-in-law, Ruth, goes with her.

B. Ruth meets Boaz (2)

Ruth gathers wheat in a field owned by Boaz. Boaz is almost Naomi's closest relative in town.

C. Ruth asks Boaz to take care of her (3)

According to Jewish law a relative like Boaz can marry Ruth and take care of her. Ruth asks him to do that.

D. Boaz marries Ruth (4)

Ruth and Boaz marry and have children.

FAQs

Q: Why were Naomi and her family in Moab?

A: There had been a famine in Judah. Naomi, her husband, and their two sons went to Moab to find food and to live.

Q: Why did Naomi need Ruth to take care of her?

A: In her day, widows were treated badly or ignored. They became poor and had very little unless a family member helped them.

LOOKOUT FOR . . .

As you read through Ruth, be on the lookout for . . .

Loyalty. Ruth shows her loyalty to Naomi by leaving her own homeland to be with Naomi.

Relationships. This story is all about relationships. Naomi to Ruth. Ruth to Boaz. Ruth and Boaz to their son.

Courage. Ruth, Naomi, and Boaz all show great courage.

SPECIAL REPORT

Kinsman Redeemer. A kinsman is a relative. A redeemer is someone who saves or rescues someone else. According to Jewish laws, if a woman's husband died, the husband's next closest relative had to take care of the woman. Boaz was a relative of Ruth, but not the next closest relative. There was one other that was closer. That is why in chapter four, Boaz talks to another man about marrying Ruth. According to the custom, if that man did not want to take the responsibility, then Boaz could step in.

Boaz offered the responsibility to this relative, but the relative refused. This meant that Boaz could marry Ruth, take care of her, and become her Kinsman Redeemer.

STUDY QUESTIONS

- Why did Naomi agree to let Ruth go with her to Bethlehem? *(Ruth 1:15-18)*
    - What did Boaz hear about Ruth? *(Ruth 2:11-12)*
    - What kind of man was Boaz? *(Ruth 2:19-20)*
    - How did God bless Ruth, Boaz, and Naomi? *(Ruth 4:13-17)*

1 SAMUEL

WHY THIS BOOK?

The book of 1 Samuel is named after a man who was last, first, and best—all rolled into one. Samuel was the last of the judges of Israel. He was the first of the school of prophets after Moses. He was also one of the best of all the prophets of Israel. In addition, Samuel was a priest.

During Samuel's leadership, the people of Israel decided they did not want a spiritual leader. They wanted a king like all the nations around them. Samuel tried to tell them all the problems and trouble they would have if they had a king. But the people would not listen. They wanted a king anyway. So even though it was not his first choice for them, God let the people have a king.

Saul became the first king of the Israelites. Samuel was the priest who anointed him. This history book of Israel records Saul's good start, his disobedience to God, and his failure. Other important stories of Israel included in 1 Samuel are David and Goliath, David's friendship with Jonathan, Saul's attempts to kill David, and Saul's death.

VITAL STATS/OUTLINE

A. Samuel as a child and judge *(1–8)*

Hannah prays for a child. God gives her Samuel. Samuel grows up in the Temple and becomes a great prophet. The elders of Israel ask for a king, and Samuel warns them of the dangers in following a person instead of God.

B. Saul's rise to power *(9–17)*

Samuel anoints Saul as Israel's first king. Saul wins some victories but also makes some mistakes.

C. Saul's decline and David's struggle *(18–31)*

Saul begins to fail as a leader. Samuel anoints David as the future king. David kills Goliath. At first Saul and David are friends, and Saul's son is David's best friend. But then Saul gets jealous of David because the people like David a lot. By the time of Saul's death, Saul considers David an enemy.

FAQs

Q: How could Samuel have so many important jobs?

A: Samuel's mother, Hannah, had asked God for a son. She promised to give him back to the Lord to serve him. Ever since he was a young child, Samuel was in training to serve God. His heart was open to the Lord, and God used him in many ways.

Q: Why did the Israelites want a king?

A: Samuel was getting old, and his sons did not follow his example in serving the Lord. In fact, they were very bad leaders. The people used this as an excuse to have a king. God said that the people were rejecting God as their king.

Q: What kind of man was Saul?

A: Saul was tall and handsome, the son of a wealthy man. He was humble at first but became proud and jealous of David later. He also began to pick and choose when he would obey God.

LOOKOUT FOR . . .

As you read through 1 Samuel, be on the lookout for . . .
Saul. There are times when Saul follows God, and there are

other times when he definitely does not.

Faithful friendships. Friendships like Jonathan and David's teach us how to be good friends.

God's leadership. God leads Samuel to both David and Saul so that he will choose the right king.

SPECIAL REPORT

Philistines. The Philistine people probably lived in the plains of Palestine. We may have even gotten the word "Palestine" from the word "Philistine."

These people were more technically advanced than the Hebrews. They worked with metal in a way the Hebrews did not understand yet. This gave the Philistines an advantage in battle. Perhaps the most famous Philistine was Goliath. Goliath, for all his might and metal, was killed by a shepherd boy with a sling, proving once again that when God is on your side, anything can happen.

STUDY QUESTIONS

• What was so bad about having a king in Israel? *(1 Samuel 8:10-20)*

• What did Saul do that made God take away his kingdom?
(1 Samuel 13:7-14)

• How did Saul's servants describe David?
(1 Samuel 16:18-19)

• Why were King Saul and his soldiers afraid of Goliath?
(1 Samuel 17:4-11)

• Why didn't David kill King Saul when he had the chance?
(1 Samuel 26:5-11)

2 SAMUEL

WHY THIS BOOK?

David's life was so important to Israel that the whole book of 2 Samuel is filled with his stories. In fact, almost 3,000 years after it was written, people still read 2 Samuel to learn from this hero.

Most people would think that David should have been glad when King Saul was finally killed in battle. But David mourned for his king and for his friend Jonathan.

The book of 2 Samuel tells how David became king over Judah and then over all of Israel. Since David followed God's ways in ruling his people, God made David successful. His people loved him and were devoted to him.

David was a good king and military leader. But he made mistakes as a father. Sometimes he did not discipline his children very well. That caused him a lot of grief.

David was far from perfect. He committed the very serious sins of adultery, deceit, and murder. But when the prophet Nathan told David he was guilty, King David admitted his sin and repented. God forgave David, but 2 Samuel records the life-long consequences that David and his family suffered.

2 Samuel

VITAL STATS/OUTLINE

A. David becomes king *(1–10)*

David becomes the official king. Even though Saul tried to kill David, David honors the memory of Saul and his son, Jonathan. David transfers the Ark of the Covenant to the Temple in Jerusalem.

B. David's sin *(11–18)*

David sins with another man's wife. Then he has her husband killed. His life is never the same as he and his family have to live with the results of what he has done.

C. David restores his kingdom *(19–24)*

David has a small militia of mighty men who show their loyalty over and over again. Unfortunately, David counts the men of Israel to prepare for war and lets the numbers go to his head, and God disciplines him for his sin of pride.

FAQs

Q: How do we know that David was sorry King Saul was killed?

A: David mourned and fasted because of his grief. He also wrote a lament, or sad song, about King Saul and Jonathan.

Q. What happened to King Saul's family?

A: David showed respect to Saul's other son who was king for a short while. He also was kind to

Jonathan's son Mephibosheth. He gave Mephibosheth all of Saul's land and let him eat at the king's table.

Q: If David was sorry for his sin, how come God still punished him?

A: God does not take sin lightly. Most of the time sin affects many people, not just the ones who do the wrong. By giving in to temptation, David set a bad example for his sons and everyone else.

LOOKOUT FOR . . .

As you read through 2 Samuel, be on the lookout for . . .

Decisions. David has to make many decisions as king. Most are wise but some are foolish.

Consequences. David makes a few very bad choices. Those choices have consequences, or results, that David has to endure, especially in his family life.

Crimes. There are several crimes recorded in 2 Samuel.

Kindness. Despite his mistakes, David shows great kindness to several people—far more than people expect of him.

SPECIAL REPORT

Ark of the Lord. The Ark of the Lord (also called the Ark of God, and the Ark of the Covenant) traveled with the Israelites in all of their journeys. The word "ark" is the same word used for a coffin or mummy case. It was like a traveling museum. Inside were the tablets on which the Ten Commandments were written. At one time there was manna and Aaron's wooden staff inside also. It was David who finally put the Ark in the Temple.

The Ark was a sacred object, so God gave very strict rules about how it was to be cared for. Normally, no one was even to touch it, not even by accident. For example, when David was moving the Ark into Jerusalem, a man named Uzzah simply touched it and fell down dead. Today, the location of the Ark is a mystery; it may have been destroyed long ago.

STUDY QUESTIONS

• What special promise did God make to David?
(2 Samuel 7:8-16)

• How did the prophet Nathan get David's attention about his sin with Bathsheba? (2 Samuel 12:1-7)

• How did God punish David for his sin? (2 Samuel 12:13-14)

• What kind of men followed King David? (2 Samuel 23:8-23)

I KINGS

WHY THIS BOOK?

The glorious kingdom that David ruled grew even bigger when his son Solomon reigned. First Kings tells how Solomon humbly asked God for wisdom to rule. God answered his request and said he would receive riches and power too. Solomon knew all about animals, plants, and how to construct buildings. God allowed him to build the beautiful Temple in Jerusalem. People traveled great distances to Jerusalem to hear the wisdom of Solomon. But Solomon, like his father, forgot God's command not to have many wives *(Deuteronomy 17:17)*. And the wives he married worshiped idols. They stole Solomon's heart away from the Lord, just as God warned would happen.

The rest of this book tells of the dividing of the nation of Israel into two kingdoms. They were Israel (the 10 northern tribes) and Judah (the two southern tribes of Judah and Benjamin). Idol worship became a constant problem for the people as they turned from the Lord.

But God did not desert his people. He sent the prophet Elijah to show the people that the Lord is the true God. No matter how wicked the people were, God was always faithful in having someone point the way back to God. The book of 1 Kings is filled with examples of people who disobeyed God and those who obeyed him.

VITAL STATS/OUTLINE

A. The rise of Solomon's kingdom *(1–10)*

God offers Solomon anything and is pleased when Solomon asks for wisdom instead of riches or power. Solomon builds the Temple and becomes powerful and rich as well as wise.

B. The kingdom is divided *(11–12)*

After Solomon dies, the kingdom divides into northern and southern kingdoms.

C. Two kingdoms, two kings *(13–22)*

Evil King Ahab lives a life of wickedness. Elijah and Elisha prophesy to God's people.

FAQs

Q: Since David had so many sons, how did Solomon become king?

A: Solomon was the one David chose to be king. Bathsheba reminded David that he had promised her that Solomon would be king. Also the Lord chose Solomon and had promised to bless him *(1 Chronicles 22:9-10)*.

Q: How did God talk to Solomon about his request?

A: God spoke to Solomon in a dream and told him to ask for whatever he wanted. God was pleased with Solomon's request for wisdom.

Q: If Solomon made mistakes about his wives, was his wisdom any good?

A: While Solomon followed the Lord, his nation enjoyed peace, security, and prosperity.

LOOKOUT FOR . . .

As you read through 1 Kings, be on the lookout for . . .

Choices. It is easy to see in 1 Kings that the choices leaders make affect a lot of people.

Good kings. The kingdoms of Israel and Judah prosper under godly kings.

God's care. God takes care of his own children. He does that for Elijah as well as Elisha.

SPECIAL REPORT

Cedar wood. When Solomon was building the Temple he used

the very best metal, wood, and stone he could find as well as the finest craftsmen. The wood he used was the finest cedar. He often referred to the cedars of Lebanon when asking for wood.

Cedars were large evergreen trees that used to be plentiful in the Mediterranean. The wood was beautiful, distasteful to insects, and strong. It was a wonderful material to use in a building built specifically to honor God's presence because it was the best of the best. Today cedar is scarce in that area.

STUDY QUESTIONS

• How did God show that he was pleased with the Temple that Solomon built? *(1 Kings 8:10-13; 9:1-3)*

• What caused the kingdom to be divided? *(1 Kings 12:1-24)*

• King Ahab was one of the worst kings of Israel. Why? *(1 Kings 16:29-33)*

• How did Elijah prove that the Lord is the true God? *(1 Kings 18:16-40)*

2 KINGS

WHY THIS BOOK?

Second Kings continues the sad story of the divided kingdom of Israel. It tells of 12 kings in the northern kingdom (called Israel) and 16 kings in the southern kingdom (Judah). Most of the kings followed the evil path of worshiping idols and turned away from God. Only a few were called good and tried to lead their people back to God. So 2 Kings really is a sad book to read.

The northern kingdom lasted only 130 years before Assyria conquered it. But because Hezekiah and Josiah obeyed God and people repented, there was revival in Judah. God kept Judah safe for another 136 years. Finally the evil ways of the people of Judah caught up with them. God sent Nebuchadnezzar to take them away into captivity in Babylonia.

During all those years, God had his prophets warning the people to return to the Lord. Most people know about Elijah and Elisha, but there were as many as 30 other prophets also trying to turn people back toward God and his ways. God was always faithful in giving people a way to hear his word and turn back to him.

VITAL STATS/OUTLINE

A. Final work of Elijah (1–2)

Elijah is taken into heaven without dying. He passes his power on to Elisha.

B. Ministry of Elisha (3–13)

Elisha works miracles, including healing Naaman of leprosy. Many kings rule including Jehu—who killed evil Queen Jezebel and the family of Ahab—and Joash, who repairs the Temple.

C. Captivity of Israel (14–17)

Israel's kings get worse and worse as rulers. They do not obey God and eventually let Israel be captured by the Assyrians.

D. Captivity of Judah (18–25)

Judah struggles under Manasseh, sees a revival, but then is defeated.

FAQs

Q: Why did the Israelites want to worship idols?

A: They wanted to be like their neighbors, and they wanted to do the sins allowed by their neighbors' religions.

Q: Why was the prophet Elijah so special?

A: The prophet Elijah was courageous and stood up against the evil rulers Ahab and Jezebel. He challenged the prophets of Baal and showed the people that the Lord is the true God. But he also became depressed and afraid. God showed his special care for Elijah by not allowing him to die and taking him straight to heaven in a whirlwind instead.

Q: What was so good about Hezekiah and Josiah?

A: These two kings of Judah tried to restore worship of the true God. Hezekiah broke down the places of false worship and destroyed idols. Josiah read God's Word to the people and promised to obey it. The people followed his good example.

LOOKOUT FOR . . .

As you read through 2 Kings, be on the lookout for . . .

Kingdoms. There is a big change happening in Israel during this time. Kingdoms are shifting and becoming parts of other kingdoms. Kings change often.

Revivals. Israel and Judah have periods of revival or coming back to God. The problem is that before each revival, they fall away from God.

Pride. Pride is often a problem in Israel. Naaman struggles with it. The kings of Israel are often so conceited that they feel no need for God's help. Foreign kings definitely feel that way.

SPECIAL REPORT

Leprosy. Leprosy was a serious skin disease. It was contagious and anyone who got it had to leave home and even go to another city. It meant losing the means to work and live with family. In 2 Kings 5 a man named Naaman was healed of leprosy by washing in the Jordan River. Jesus healed people of leprosy on more than one occasion.

Many Old Testament laws taught people how to deal with leprosy. There were certain ways that the leper (someone with leprosy) was to be treated and certain ways to clean his home after he moved out of it. Leprosy was such a serious condition that when a leper saw other people coming down the road, he had to yell "Unclean! Unclean!" to warn them not to come near.

It was an amazing thing, then, since leprosy was so horrible, that Naaman was almost unwilling to wash in a river to cure himself. If he had not been so proud, he would have jumped right in.

STUDY QUESTIONS

- What did Elisha want Elijah to do for him? (2 Kings 2:9-13)
- How did Elisha show that God loves even Israel's enemies? (2 Kings 5:1-16)
- How did King Josiah find the Book of the Law? (2 Kings 22:1-20)
- What happened to Jerusalem when the Babylonians captured it? (2 Kings 25:8-10)

1 CHRONICLES

WHY THIS BOOK?

People like to know where they came from and who their ancestors were. The book of 1 Chronicles gives long lists of people from Adam to Zerubbabel. It shows how God worked in his people's lives for many generations. There are lists of kings, members of particular tribes, Temple musicians, priests, people who returned from exile in Babylonia, and David's mighty men.

First Chronicles goes along with 2 Samuel. It fills in many of the details. It was written after the exile of the Israelites. It doesn't focus on all the kings of Israel and their battles. Instead, it shows how David helped establish worship in the nation of Israel. It talks about David taking the Ark to Jerusalem and preparing to build the Temple. Reading 1 Chronicles is a good way to see the history of worship in Israel and Judah.

VITAL STATS/OUTLINE

A. The genealogies (1–8)

These lists give the histories of each of the families of Jacob's twelve sons.

B. Taking back the land (9)

The Israelites had been captives in Babylonia. Now they return to their homeland.

C. Reign of David *(10–21)*

David is king of Israel. He returns the Ark of the Covenant to the Temple and wins many military victories.

D. Preparation for the Temple *(22–29)*

God does not want David to build the Temple, but he lets him get all the materials and workers together so that Solomon can oversee the building project later.

FAQs

Q: What's so important about this book?

A: This book was useful for the people returning to Jerusalem after being in exile in Babylon. It helped them know how God had worked in their nation. It would encourage them to trust God and obey him.

Q: What message does this book have for people who are not Jewish?

A: First Chronicles can remind all believers in Christ of their spiritual "grandparents."

Q: How come David only planned the Temple? Why did not he build it?

1 Chronicles

A: David wanted to build the Temple *(1 Chronicles 22:8; 28:3)* but the Lord would not let him. God said David was a "warrior" who "shed much blood." So God let Solomon, who lived in peace, build the Temple.

LOOKOUT FOR . . .

As you read through 1 Chronicles, be on the lookout for . . .

Emotions. First Chronicles tells about the emotions of the people in the story. David is fearful at times. At other times he is joyful and full of praise. These people are like you in that they have good days and bad days.

Prayers. First Chronicles includes several of David's prayers.

Lists. First Chronicles gives not only lists of history or descendants (genealogies) but also lists of warriors and leaders.

SPECIAL REPORT

Genealogies. The word "genealogy" is like the word "generations." Sometimes, in fact, instead of calling a list a "genealogy," the Bible says "These are the generations of . . . ." A genealogy is a list of people in a bloodline. It is the history of a family.

Genealogies can be tricky because not all are the same. Different genealogies have different purposes. For example, the genealogies in Genesis 4 tell a lot about the people's work. Not all genealogies are like that. And one genealogy of Jesus' ancestors goes back through Joseph's family, while another goes back through Mary's family. So they have different names in them.

First Chronicles has the major genealogy tables of the Old Testament. These lists help us remember that these people we read about were real people with families.

STUDY QUESTIONS

• What lesson did David learn from moving the Ark of God? (1 Chronicles 13:3-14; 15:1-2)

• What did David say about God's promise to him? (1 Chronicles 17:16-27)

• How did David help his son Solomon? (1 Chronicles 22:2-19)

2 CHRONICLES

WHY THIS BOOK?

Peoples' lives are filled with many details. Second Chronicles helps fill in the facts left out of 1 and 2 Kings. It gives more information about the southern kingdom of Judah. In some ways it seems to ignore the northern kingdom. It is the second part of Chronicles, as its name says. (It used to be that 1 and 2 Chronicles were one book.)

Second Chronicles was written to all of God's people to show the importance of worship. It also tells of spiritual revivals that took place in Judah. Second Chronicles gives the history of Solomon's reign as king. It goes down through the time that the people of Judah were captured and taken to Babylonia. By then, the people had stopped worshiping the Lord.

He allowed the Babylonians to destroy the beautiful Temple that Solomon had built.

VITAL STATS/OUTLINE

A. Solomon's reign (1–9)

Solomon asks for wisdom, builds and dedicates the Temple, and gets a visit from the queen of Sheba.

B. Kings of Judah (10–36)

The kingdom divides and Judah is ruled by 19 kings (and a queen), from Rehoboam to Zedekiah. But at God's command, Babylon puts an end to it all.

FAQs

Q: Why did God make Solomon so wise?

A: Solomon asked God to make him wise. He did not ask for riches or fame. That pleased God. So God gave him the wisdom he requested, plus riches and honor.

Q: Just how rich was Solomon?

A: During Solomon's reign, his silver and gold were as "common as stones"!

Q: What actually happened to make the kingdom be divided?

A: Solomon's son Rehoboam did not listen to the good advice of the elders who had helped Solomon. He listened to the young men who said he should be even harder on the people. That made most of the people very angry. So the ten tribes of the north followed another king instead of Rehoboam.

2 Chronicles

LOOKOUT FOR . . .

As you read through 2 Chronicles, be on the lookout for . . .

Wars and invasions. This is a violent time in Israel's history. There are many mentions in 2 Chronicles of troops and invasions and out-and-out wars. Usually these conflicts come when the nation is caught up in sin.

Acts of unfaithfulness. Notice how the behavior of the Israelites changes when they drift away from God. They do not just change their minds, they change their whole way of living. Worshiping God affects the way we live our lives, too.

Revivals. There are several revivals in this section of history. Whenever a good and righteous king reigns, he leads the people back to the worship of the one true God. Unfortunately, the people fall back into their old ways as soon as a new king comes along.

SPECIAL REPORT

Asherah. Asherah was a goddess of the Phoenicians and Syrians. The Israelites began to worship Asherah when they fell into idolatry. She was also called Ashtoreth, Astarte, Anath, or Lady of the Sea. She was often worshiped by the same people who worshiped Baal.

Asherah was a goddess

of fertility. Often that means that the worship of this goddess included sexual immorality. The pictures and statues of the goddess would have been something you might call "bad" or "dirty" because they had to do with actions that God calls sin.

Chronicles mentions "Asherah poles," which were objects used in worship that were probably statues that were supposed to look like this goddess. Whenever Israel was in a revival they would tear down the Asherah poles. Whenever Israel was in rebellion they would put Asherah poles up.

STUDY QUESTIONS

• How did God keep his promise to David?
(2 Chronicles 6:3-11)

• What was Solomon's kingdom like? (2 Chronicles 9:13-28)

• How did God react when his people turned from their sin?
(2 Chronicles 12:1-8; 33:10-13)

• Why did God punish his people? (2 Chronicles 36:15-16)

• How did God use a pagan king to fulfill prophecy?
(2 Chronicles 36:22-23)

EZRA

WHY THIS BOOK?

Does God use only people who believe in him? The book of Ezra shows how the Lord directs world events to fit his will. God had promised his people they would be in captivity in Babylonia for 70 years. When that time was up, God moved the heart of King Cyrus to allow the people to return to Jerusalem.

The book of Ezra describes two groups of Israelites who returned to their beloved country. The first group was led by Zerubbabel. Those who went are listed by family name. Over forty-two thousand people returned with this first group. With Cyrus' permission they began rebuilding the Temple soon after they got back to Jerusalem. Cyrus also allowed others to give them silver, gold, and supplies they would need for the task. But not everyone was happy about this event. Some people tried to discourage the Jews from working. They accused God's people of being rebellious and corrupt.

A second group went with Ezra 80 years later during the reign of King Artaxerxes. The work of rebuilding the Temple was done, but the people had not been obeying God at all. For example, they had married people who worshiped idols. Ezra feared for the well-being of his people. Ezra prayed and helped his people repent of their sin.

VITAL STATS/OUTLINE

A. Restoration of worship *(1–6)*

The first exiles return to Jerusalem and begin rebuilding the Temple. Enemies try to stop them, but the Temple is completed anyway.

B. Ezra's reforms *(7–10)*

Ezra arrives and urges the people to obey God with their whole hearts. The people respond and change the way they are living.

FAQs

Q: Who was Ezra?

A: Ezra was a priest and a scribe. He may be the one who wrote most of 1 and 2 Chronicles, Ezra, Nehemiah, and Psalm 119. He loved God and wanted his people to obey God. He worked hard to help them understand and obey God's Word.

Q: Why did some of the older people cry when the foundation of the Temple was laid?

A: The older people had seen the glory of Solomon's Temple, and they knew this one would not be as beautiful as the original one.

Q: Why didn't Ezra want to ask the king for protection for the trip back to Jerusalem?

A: Ezra had told King Artaxerxes that the Lord takes care of those who trust in him. So Ezra prayed and fasted for God's protection.

LOOKOUT FOR . . .

As you read through Ezra, be on the lookout for . . .

Exiles. Exiles are people who are forced to leave their country. In this story they are Israelites who have been captives in Persia and are coming back home. They are coming back to Israel in groups.

Lists. Ezra gives several lists: lists of supplies, lists of people returning home, and lists of people caught in sin.

Memos and proclamations. Ezra gives us the exact words of several kings. They send out official documents, but since they do not have paper copiers, one person reads the documents to everyone

else. There are messages from three kings: Cyrus, Darius, and Artaxerxes.

SPECIAL REPORT

Intermarriage. One of the biggest problems the Jews faced at this time was marriage to people who did not love God. God told them not to do it. The biggest reason was idol worship. The nations around Israel all worshiped false gods. Whenever a Jew married someone who loved idols, they tended to worship those idols instead of the one true God. This was something God just would not put up with.

Ezra confronted a long list of priests who had married pagan wives. Ezra went so far as to list every man. It took three months to straighten it all out. Out of all those men, only two refused to obey the Lord.

STUDY QUESTIONS

• How did God use King Cyrus to help the Jewish exiles? (*Ezra 1:2-11*)

• What kind of problem did the Jews have to overcome while rebuilding the Temple? (*Ezra 4:1-5*)

NEHEMIAH

WHY THIS BOOK?

Prayer and action are the key words for the book of Nehemiah. The man Nehemiah was an Israelite living in exile in Persia (old Babylonia). He was the cup-bearer to King Artaxerxes. That was an important job. He heard that the walls of Jerusalem were still broken down after many years. The news made him very sad. He wept. He mourned and fasted. He prayed to the Lord. Then he bravely asked Artaxerxes if he could go to Jerusalem and rebuild the walls.

This book shows how Nehemiah prayed, planned, and worked hard. He encouraged the people living in Jerusalem. They needed a strong leader to help them do the work. There were enemies who did not want the walls rebuilt. Nehemiah had to post guards. Many of the men worked with one hand while holding a weapon in the other.

Some men even tried to scare Nehemiah. But he continued trusting God and doing the work.

This book tells about the physical work that Nehemiah and the people did. It also tells about their devotion to God. Ezra was with Nehemiah. They worked together. Ezra read the Book of the Law to the people and helped them learn how God wanted them to live.

The book of Nehemiah tells of the building of the walls of Jerusalem and the revival of God's people.

VITAL STATS/OUTLINE

A. Nehemiah returns to Jerusalem *(1–2)*

Nehemiah returns and inspects the Jerusalem walls.

B. Rebuilding the walls *(3–7)*

The work begins with enemies trying to stand in the way. The walls are rebuilt in just 52 days.

C. Revival *(8–10)*

Ezra, the priest, reads the Book of the Law, and the people repent.

D. Lists and genealogies *(11:1–12:26)*

The people return to Jerusalem and to their homes, organized by families.

E. Dedicating and reforming *(12:27–13:31)*

The people dedicate the walls, and Nehemiah begins to change the way they do some things.

FAQs

Q: What was so important about being a cup-bearer?

A: The cup-bearer was a highly trusted attendant of the king. He tasted the king's wine first to make sure it was good—and not poisoned! Then he gave it to the king.

Nehemiah

Q: Why were the walls of Jerusalem still broken down?

A: People who were not Israelites settled in the land of Judah when the Israelites were taken captive. Those people did not want the Jews (Israelites) to build up their city again.

Q: What did the Jews do when Nehemiah wanted to rebuild the walls?

A: They were glad to have a leader. They got busy and started working right away.

LOOKOUT FOR . . .

As you read through Nehemiah, be on the lookout for . . .

Confessions. When the people read the law, they are reminded of their sin. Then they confess their sins to God so they can ask his forgiveness. Obstacles. The book of Nehemiah is a story of overcoming obstacles (things that get in your way). Nehemiah has a long journey to make. Some people try to stop the building of the walls. Some of the people have disagreements. And some of the Jews have a lot of sin in their lives.

Details. Nehemiah has a lot of small but important things to take care of, so he gets real organized. In fact, this book is a great example of organization.

SPECIAL REPORT

Festival of Shelters. In reading the Scriptures Ezra realized that the people were supposed to hold a celebration called the Festival of Shelters. This festival involved making temporary shelters or booths to live in for seven days. Ezra and the people were so excited about obeying God that they went right out and collected branches and leaves to make their shelters.

The Festival of Shelters (also called booths or tabernacles) was the last of the sacred festivals in the calendar year. It began five days after the Day of Atonement (Leviticus 23:34) and lasted seven days. This festival had two purposes. First, it celebrated the end of the harvest. Second, it reminded the people of the Exodus, when their ancestors had to live in tents.

STUDY QUESTIONS

• How did Nehemiah answer Sanballat and Tobiah when they mocked and ridiculed him? (Nehemiah 2:19-20)

• What did Nehemiah and the other Jews do when they were threatened? (Nehemiah 4)

• How did the people react to Ezra's reading of God's Word? (Nehemiah 8:1-12)

ESTHER

WHY THIS BOOK?

The book of Esther is one of only two books in the Bible named after a woman (the other is Ruth). It tells the story of a young Jewish woman becoming a queen of Persia. This unusual event was part of God's plan to save the Jewish people throughout the entire kingdom of King Xerxes (Ahasuerus).

Haman, the king's prime minister, hated Jews, especially Mordecai. Haman plotted to have them all killed. He did not know that Queen Esther was Jewish. Mordecai was Esther's cousin and adopted father. He told Esther of the plot and encouraged her to help her people.

But just because she was queen did not mean Esther could do whatever she wanted. No one, not even a queen, could speak to the king unless he gave the invitation. Esther told Mordecai to gather all the Jews in the city to fast and pray for her. Then she would approach the king.

It took great courage and wisdom for Esther to find a way to speak to the king and turn the evil plot back on Haman. But God helped Esther, and her people were saved! It is an amazing story of God's work through God's people.

VITAL STATS/OUTLINE

A. Queen Vashti is dethroned (1)

Because the queen will not appear at the king's party, she loses her position as queen.

B. Esther becomes queen (2)

Esther's cousin enters her in the contest for a queen to replace Vashti. Esther goes through a year of beauty treatments, then wins the king's heart and becomes his wife. She does not tell him she is a Jew because the Jews are captives.

C. Haman's decree and destruction (3–7)

Haman starts to resent Mordecai because Mordecai does not show enough respect to him. (Haman does not deserve the respect.) Haman plans not only to do away with Mordecai, but also to get rid of all the Jews. But Esther is one step ahead of him and asks the king to protect her people. Haman loses favor with the king and is executed.

D. The Jews celebrate their deliverance (8–9)

Esther instructs the people to celebrate the feast of Purim to remember God's deliverance.

E. Mordecai is recognized (10)

The king realizes what a valuable man Mordecai is and makes him an important man in the kingdom.

FAQs

Q: How did Esther become queen?

A: The king wanted a new queen. He made all the beautiful young women come into his harem. Esther won his favor and he chose her as his queen.

Q: How come no one knew Esther was Jewish?

A: Mordecai had told Esther not to tell her nationality or her background.

Q: Why did Haman hate Mordecai so much?

A: Haman was a descendant of the royal line of the Amalekites, ancient enemies of the Jews. Mordecai refused to bow down to Haman, even though Haman had been specially honored by the king.

Q: Why was it such a big deal for Esther to talk to the king?

A: The law said that no one could approach the king unless the king invited the person to come. Anyone who disobeyed this law and came uninvited was put to death. Only if the king held out his golden scepter would the person be spared.

LOOKOUT FOR . . .

As you read through Esther, be on the lookout for . . .

Opportunities. Esther, Mordecai, and Haman all have opportunities to do something, some good and some bad. Watch what they do with their opportunities.

Deceit and pride. A lot of Haman's actions come out of pride and deceit. Do not be fooled!

Social customs. There are many social customs of the Persians in this book. For instance, the beauty contest for queen, the way people get to talk to the king, dinner arrangements, and festivals all say a little bit about the people of that time and place.

SPECIAL REPORT

Gallows. When Haman was planning for Mordecai's death, he built a "gallows" in his front yard. A gallows is a wooden platform with a pole and a rope hanging down. It is used to hang a person. But the Persians did not hang people. They had a different form of execution— they would impale people on poles. The word for "gallows" here in Esther means "pole," so Haman's gallows was probably a pole on which he planned to have Mordecai impaled.

If you think that sounds horrible, you are right. This was a very violent time in history. The Persians of that time did not honor human life as much as we do in our country today.

STUDY QUESTIONS

• What did Haman do when he found out Mordecai was a Jew? (*Esther 3:5-14*)

• What happened to make Haman honor Mordecai? (*Esther 6:1-13*)

• What happened to Haman when the king understood his plot? (**Esther 7:9-10**)

• How did Esther and Mordecai change Haman's message so the Jews would not be destroyed? (*Esther 8:7-8; 11-17*)

JOB

WHY THIS BOOK?

Good people never have problems, right? Wrong! The book of Job is about a very good man named Job. God described him as "blameless," a man who loved God and "stayed away from evil." But Job had more trouble in one day than most people have in a lifetime. In fact, Job had so much trouble that no one could comfort him.

God pointed out Job as a good example of a follower of God. But Satan (the Accuser) said Job just loved God for what he could get for himself. Not so, said God, and he gave Satan permission to test Job.

In one day Job's 10 children were killed, his servants were killed, and all his wealth was destroyed or stolen. Satan expected Job to curse God. Instead, Job worshiped God!

Next Satan wanted to test Job by hurting his body. God gave Satan permission to hurt Job but not kill him. Satan caused painful sores all over Job's body.

Job felt miserable. He became discouraged. He could not figure out why God was allowing all this trouble. But he never cursed God.

Some of Job's friends visited him. At first they just sat with him and kept him company. Later they argued with him that all his trouble was caused by his sin. But Job had not sinned, and he knew it.

God did not answer Job's questions. But he helped Job see that God is in control—even when bad things happen to good people.

VITAL STATS/OUTLINE

A. Satan tests Job *(1–2)*
Satan comes to God and asks permission to test Job.
B. Job and his friends discuss his suffering *(3–31)*

Job and three friends talk about his suffering and why it is happening. For the most part, their answers upset Job instead of comfort him. They think Job has done something wrong to deserve what is happening.

C. Elihu speaks *(32–37)*
Elihu does not blame Job like the other three do.
D. God speaks *(38:1–42:9)*
God speaks to Job and sets the record straight. He shows Job how wrong his three friends are.
E. Job's reply and conclusion *(42:10-17)*

Job

Job admits that God's ways are hard to understand. But he also affirms that God is good. God corrects Job's friends and then blesses Job with more than he had before.

FAQs

Q: Why did Satan have power to hurt Job?

A: God let Satan do it. God gave Satan special permission to test Job's faith.

Q: Does Satan cause all suffering?

A: No. People can make good or bad choices. Bad choices can cause trouble for them and others. Also, sometimes God allows and uses hard things to help our faith grow stronger.

Q: Why did Job's friends think he sinned?

A: They thought good things happen only to good people and bad things happen only to bad people. Even Job was confused. He knew he had not sinned, so he did not know why he was "being punished."

LOOKOUT FOR . . .

As you read through Job, be on the lookout for . . .

Losses. Job loses almost everything. Can you think of anything he does not lose?

Arguments. As Job and his friends talk back and forth, they are almost arguing, not because they are angry but because they are trying to figure all this out.

Job's defense. Job is brave enough to stand up to his friends. He has done nothing wrong to deserve such suffering, and he is brave enough to say it.

SPECIAL REPORT

Suffering. To suffer means to hurt, or to have bad things happen to you. People have struggled with suffering since the beginning of time. The people of Israel complained when they suffered in the wilderness even though they were free from slavery in Egypt.

Often people think that suffering is a punishment from God for doing wrong. All of Job's friends thought that. Even Jesus' disciples thought that. But no one can know why God allows this or that bad thing to happen. And we should never assume that we know.

In John 9:1-3 Jesus and his disciples meet a man that has been blind from birth. The disciples' first question is, "Why did this happen? Did this man sin or did his parents?" Jesus tells his disciples that the man's blindness is not a punishment from God at all. It is an opportunity for people to see him healed by God and be amazed at God's power and love.

Bad things happen to people. Even though we may want to blame someone or ask God why, we may not get an answer.

Job

Whenever we suffer we should do what Job did. We should praise God because we know that he is with us and has a plan for our lives.

STUDY QUESTIONS

- What poor advice did Job's wife give him? *(Job 2:9)*
- What effect did God's words have on Job? *(Job 42:1-6)*
- How did God feel about Job's friends? *(Job 42:7-9)*
- What did God do for Job after Job prayed for his friends? *(Job 42:10-17)*

PSALMS

WHY THIS BOOK?

Sometimes people do not say what they are really thinking. But the Psalms are not like that—they say it all just like it is. They have joyful praise to the Lord. They have mournful sorrow for sin. They have prayer for direction and comfort. They have requests to punish people who reject God.

Some psalms cry out for help in hard places. Others ask God for daily needs to be met. There are prayers for forgiveness.

The psalms were written by different people. Some are meant for public worship. Some are private thoughts written when people were discouraged.

There are 150 psalms. Some were written by David, Asaph, the sons of Korah, Solomon, Heman, Ethan, and Moses. Some have no known author. All teach many things—about God the Creator, his power, his faithfulness. Many speak of Christ in the future.

Psalms are actually songs to be sung. The book of Psalms was the hymn book of the Jews. Over the years, many psalms have been put to different music for Christians to sing.

Psalms

VITAL STATS/OUTLINE

The book of Psalms is divided into five smaller books. Within each book are a variety of subjects including praise, repentance, worship, prayer and others.

A. Book One *(1–41)*
B. Book Two *(42–72)*
C. Book Three *(73–89)*
D. Book Four *(90–106)*
E. Book Five *(107–150)*

FAQs

Q: If the psalms are songs, why don't they rhyme?

A: Hebrew poetry is different from English poetry. It does not rhyme. Instead, the second line often repeats the first line in different words. In fact, almost all Hebrew poetry uses two lines to make its point. The first line says something, and then the second line says it again in a different way. Sometimes each line begins with the next letter of the alphabet.

Q: Why did David pray for God to punish his enemies?

A: David and the other writers of the psalms were people just like you, and they told God how they really felt. They also knew that God is in control, so they asked him to change things. That's exactly how we should pray too.

LOOKOUT FOR . . .

As you read through Psalms, be on the lookout for . . .

Instruments. The Psalms mention many musical instruments such as lyres and tambourines. Many of the instruments you read about in Psalms are still in use today.

Composers. Many Psalms have a byline. You will see different names, but many are by King David.

Praise. A big theme of the Psalms is praise. Songs or psalms help us joyfully praise God for our lives and the good things in them.

SPECIAL REPORT

Musical instruments. There are many musical instruments listed in the Psalms. You'll recognize some of them, such as bells and cymbals and flutes. But even though some of the names are the same, the instruments have changed.

The Jews used a tambourine in their worship services. These tambourines did not have the metal pieces along the side that made the jingle noises, though. They were more like small, hand-held drums. The harps were smaller than the harps we see today and had only ten strings. The trumpets were long ram horns or metal horns, but they did not have pistons to push with your fingers to make different sounds.

There were also instruments with completely different names, but we still have something like them. Sistrums were shakers that fit in your hand. A lyre was a small harp. It was played with a pectrum or a kind of pick.

The people of Israel used many other musical instruments too. Music has always been an important part of worship.

STUDY QUESTIONS

• How does David describe a person who pleases God? (*Psalm 15*)

• What does David say about a person who asks for God's forgiveness? (*Psalm 32*)

• What are some ways people can praise God? (*Psalm 150*)

PROVERBS

WHY THIS BOOK?

No one wants to be called foolish. The book of Proverbs can help make people wise. It is a source of wisdom. Most of it was written by Solomon, who was the wisest king of Israel. Solomon wrote these wise sayings and rules for living, especially for God's people. But God has given them to everyone who wants to know how to live wisely.

The truly wise person wants to know and love God. A wise person learns how to live peacefully with family, friends, neighbors, co-workers, and others.

The book of Proverbs is written in Hebrew poetry. It is not the kind of poetry that rhymes. Instead, the lines are in couplets, or double lines. The lines are joined with words such as "but" or "and." For example, Proverbs 10:8 says,

The wise are glad to be instructed,
but babbling fools fall flat on their faces.

Proverbs covers every topic you can imagine related to living. It tells us how to use money, as well as how not to use it. It tells us the difference between foolishness and wisdom. It tells us how to succeed. It tells us what is right and what is wrong. It even tells us what God loves and hates.

Proverbs

The Proverbs are important for everyone who wants to make good decisions.

VITAL STATS/OUTLINE

This book is filled with short verses about a lot of different things. These are the general categories.

A. Advice for getting wisdom *(1–9)*

B. General instructions on righteous living *(10–16)*

C. Advice for increasing wisdom, understanding, and learning *(17–24)*

D. Instructions and warnings about rejecting the truth *(25–29)*

E. Examples of wonderful, wise, and foolish things *(30–31)*

This portion includes a famous passage on the noble wife.

FAQs

Q: Who else wrote some of the proverbs besides Solomon?

A: Other people mentioned as authors of some proverbs are Agur and Lemuel.

Q: What made Solomon so wise?

A: When Solomon began to reign as king, God asked him what he wanted. Solomon asked for wisdom. God answered his prayer.

Q: Isn't Solomon the one who was foolish about having a lot of wives?

A: Yes, but he wrote these wise sayings early in his reign, when he was still seeking wisdom from God.

LOOKOUT FOR . . .

As you read through Proverbs, be on the lookout for . . .

Lazy people. Proverbs has a lot to say about people who are not willing to work.

Wisdom. Proverbs is a book about getting wisdom and then living by it. Since God made Solomon very wise, it makes sense that Solomon would write a book about wisdom.

Family guidelines. There are many verses about how parents should treat kids and how kids should treat parents.

SPECIAL REPORT

Discipline. Proverbs has a lot to say about discipline. It says that parents should discipline kids and that people should discipline themselves and that God disciplines us. So what is discipline?

Discipline is not punishment. Punishment is something unpleasant that you receive because you did something bad. Discipline is more than that. Discipline is control for a time. A parent controls a child's life until the child learns the right way to live. God disciplines us by doing something in our life that makes us stop and think so that we can make better choices. We discipline ourselves when we control ourselves instead of doing whatever we want, whenever we want, no matter if it's right or wrong.

Proverbs says over and over again that discipline is a good thing. We should be open to it and appreciate it.

STUDY QUESTIONS

- What is the purpose of Proverbs? *(Proverbs 1:1-6)*
- Why is it important to guard your heart? *(Proverbs 4:23)*
- How did Jesus use the Proverbs? *(Proverbs 25:6-7; Luke 14:7-11)*

ECCLESIASTES

WHY THIS BOOK?

Sometimes people say that experience is the best teacher. But learning from another person's mistakes is even wiser. Solomon wrote Ecclesiastes at the end of his life. The things he wrote can help us be wise if we follow his advice.

Solomon, the most glorious king of Israel, had everything his heart could desire. But he realized that nothing can give happiness if a person doesn't know God.

Solomon, or "the preacher," said that apart from God, everything is in vain. If a person is very popular but not really a good friend, popularity is lonely. If someone has a great job but works only for himself or herself, the job has no purpose. Even fancy cars, big houses, nice clothes, pretty jewelry, money to travel, or great knowledge will not make a person happy apart from God.

God made people spiritual beings. We need to know God in order for life to have real meaning.

VITAL STATS/OUTLINE

A. Riches, success, and prosperity do not make us happy (1:1–5:13)

Solomon had all this and more, but without obeying God he

was still miserable.

B. Possessions usually make life harder rather than easier (5:14–6:12)

We think the more we have the happier we will be. But things do not bring happiness.

C. People do not know what is best for them (7–11)

Because we do not really know what is best for us, we make bad choices. We need God to help us make better choices.

D. The one way to live (12)

Fearing and obeying God is the only meaningful way to live.

FAQs

Q: What kinds of things did Solomon have?

A: Solomon was wealthy, and he had delicious food, expensive clothes, a large palace, slaves, attendants, horses and chariots, beautiful gardens with flowers, and fruit trees. He was popular. People visited him from other countries to hear his wisdom. He lived in peace and ease. He had many beautiful wives and children.

Q: Why wasn't Solomon happy?

A: Solomon forgot to stay close to the Lord. Without living for the true God, he could not find peace—no matter how much stuff he had.

LOOKOUT FOR . . .

As you read through Ecclesiastes, be on the lookout for . . .
"Under the Sun." Solomon uses this phrase a lot.

Accomplishments and riches. Solomon is not shy about telling about what he has done and gotten.

Happiness. Ecclesiastes talks about happiness more than any

other Bible book. Notice what kinds of things make people happy or unhappy.

SPECIAL REPORT

Meaninglessness (futility, vanity). Ecclesiastes talks a lot about what is meaningless. (Some other Bibles use the word "vanity" or "futile" instead of "meaningless.") The word means empty. It means something that does not even have a reason or purpose. Some Bibles use the phrase "chasing after the wind." It is silly to chase the wind because you can never catch it.

Solomon wrote this when he was old. He was probably looking back at the things that he thought were so important, but then he realized that only his relationships with people and with God were important.

Solomon wrote so much about this because he wanted his life to matter. That is how we all are. We want our lives to matter. We want to do something that is important and that makes a difference. We do not want to waste our lives. Over and over again Solomon reminds us that if we want our lives to matter we need to build a strong friendship with God and live our lives for him. Solomon also says we need to enjoy this life that God has given us. Then when we are old we will not feel like we wasted our life.

STUDY QUESTIONS

• What good advice did Solomon give to young people?
(Ecclesiastes 12:1)

• Why should people study Solomon's wise sayings?
(Ecclesiastes 12:9-11)

• What is Solomon's final, most important word of advice?
(Ecclesiastes 12:13-14)

SONG OF SONGS

WHY THIS BOOK?

Everyone wants to be loved. Wouldn't it be great if God made sure everyone was?

The Song of Songs is a love song written by King Solomon. It tells about his love for his wife and of his wife's love for him. It celebrates their love for each other and the way it brought them together. It shows that love kept them together too.

In other words, God invented the special love that makes a marriage work. In God's plan, marriage is a very big thing. It gives people companionship, pleasure, and a safe place to raise a family. This song tells about two people falling in love, marrying, and growing in their love for each other. The words are very powerful, because true love is a great thing.

VITAL STATS/OUTLINE

A. All the ways they love each other *(1:2–3:5)*

People who love each other give each other compliments. That is what these two people are doing.

B. The marriage *(3:6–5:1)*

Solomon marries his bride.

C. The wife misses her husband *(5:2–6:3)*

The woman goes searching for

her husband because she loves him so much.

    D. The beauty of the Shulammite bride *(6:4–7:9)*

    This young king talks more about how beautiful his wife is.

    E. The wonder of love *(7:10–8:14)*

FAQs

Q: Why don't we talk about the Song of Songs in Sunday school?

A: This book is a love song for people who are married.

Q: Why is this book in the Bible?

A: It shows how important it is for husbands and wives to love each other. It also shows that marriage is God's idea—and a pretty good one too!

LOOKOUT FOR . . .

As you read through Song of Songs, be on the lookout for . . .

Compliments. When people are in love, they build each other up. They cannot say enough good things about each other. That is how this couple is.

Comparisons. Often in the Song of Songs the writer compares one thing to another. He says, "She is as fair as the moon." She says, "His eyes are like doves." They find all the wonderful things around them and compare those wonderful things to the person they love.

SPECIAL REPORT

Gazelle or roe. A gazelle is the same kind of animal as the antelope or deer. It could run very fast and could live well in the desert. The animal was sure-footed and could make its way quickly over rough terrain.

The gazelle is a beautiful animal as well as a fast one. It moves with grace and elegance. That is why it is used to describe beauty in the Song of Songs.

STUDY QUESTIONS

- What's so special about love? *(Song of Songs 8:6-7)*
- What piece of advice about love did Solomon's wife have for her friends? *(Song of Songs 2:7; 3:5; 8:4)*

ISAIAH

WHY THIS BOOK?

Some people want to know the future. But many go to the wrong source to find out what is going to happen. They go to fortune-tellers. God said not to do that. Instead, the Lord sent prophets to tell the people of Israel the future.

One of the greatest prophets was Isaiah. His prophecies usually had a double message. Something would happen soon after the prophet spoke. Then a second, fuller event would take place hundreds of years later. Some of those events are still in the future. Isaiah's prophecies were written down in the book of Isaiah. Many of the things Isaiah spoke about were the coming of the Messiah, Jesus Christ. The book of Isaiah is divided into two parts. The first part was to warn Judah, Israel, and nearby pagan nations. God was going to punish them for sin. Unfortunately, the people did not pay attention to Isaiah's warnings. The second part of Isaiah is filled with words of comfort: The promise of forgiveness is found in the Messiah. People can especially find hope in this promise today.

VITAL STATS/OUTLINE

A. Judgment on Israel and Judah *(1–12)*
Israel and Judah have become sinful nations.
B. Judgment on foreign nations *(13–23)*
Prophecies against Babylon, Assyria, Philistia, Moab, Damascus, Egypt, and Tyre.
C. Prophecies of end times *(24–35)*
Isaiah describes the great tribulation as well as the future reign of Christ.
D. Historical accounts *(36–39)*
Sennacherib's invasion, Hezekiah's sickness, and the arrival of the Babylonian captors.
E. The Book of Consolation *(40–66)*
Prophecies of redemption and restoration. These prophecies bring comfort to the people who are in exile in Babylonia.

FAQs

Q: Who was Isaiah?
A: Isaiah was an Israelite prophet, the son of Amoz. Isaiah married a prophetess. They had two sons. Isaiah was probably reared in an upper class home. He preached mainly to Judah. He was a

writer and spokesman to four kings (not counting the Assyrian king Sennacherib).

Q: How did Isaiah know he was supposed to be a prophet?

A: Isaiah saw the Lord on his throne in the Temple. When Isaiah saw his sinfulness next to God's holiness, he was afraid. But God forgave him. Then God asked who would go to the people for him. Isaiah said he would go.

Q: Why did God want Isaiah to be a prophet?

A: The people were disobeying God. They were worshiping idols and even sacrificing their children to the false gods. God was going to punish his people for their wickedness. But he wanted Isaiah to get their attention so they would turn back to him and not suffer.

LOOKOUT FOR . . .

As you read through Isaiah, be on the lookout for . . .

Descriptions of God. Isaiah uses many titles and descriptions for God. Each is filled with awe and respect.

Salvation. Isaiah is the great "salvation" prophet. He explains salvation in many ways, including word pictures involving everything from water to white wool.

The Messiah. Isaiah says a lot about the Messiah, including one of the most famous passages of all, chapter 53.

SPECIAL REPORT

Babylon. Babylon was the capital of a country with almost the same name, Babylonia. One of Babylon's most famous rulers was Nebuchadnezzar. During his reign there were more than 50 temples to false gods. He is probably the ruler who built the famous hanging gardens that became one of the seven wonders of the world.

Some of the Israelites taken into exile were taken to Babylon. Daniel was one of the most famous Israelite residents of the capital city. He was there when Nebuchadnezzar, Darius, and Cyrus were rulers. Eventually the Jews were allowed to return to their homeland. After some time had passed, Babylon began to decline. Today it is just an abandoned city buried under sand in the desert of Iraq. Some parts of it have been dug up, but none of its glory remains.

STUDY QUESTIONS

- What was it like for Isaiah to see the Lord? *(Isaiah 6:1-8)*
- What are some of the most well-known prophecies about the Messiah? *(Isaiah 7:14; 9:6-7; 53:1-12)*

JEREMIAH

WHY THIS BOOK?

Bad news is not what most people want to hear. But the prophet Jeremiah had a lot of bad news to tell his people. They were neglecting the true God and following false gods. The Lord told Jeremiah to warn them of coming punishment. Jeremiah wrote God's warnings and promises in a book.

Jeremiah spoke to ordinary people, false prophets, priests, and kings. Baruch, his secretary, wrote down the words that Jeremiah received from the Lord. But the people would not listen to Jeremiah. One king even burned up the scroll on which Jeremiah had written God's message. Jeremiah and Baruch just made another one.

The punishment that was coming was fierce.

It was so bad that God told Jeremiah not to marry. God did not want Jeremiah to have a wife and children who would suffer the terrible times that were coming.

Jeremiah prophesied for 40 years. Very few people listened to him in all that time. He was rejected by almost everyone.

But Jeremiah's prophecies came true, just as God had said they would. Jerusalem was destroyed by the Babylonian king, Nebuchadnezzar, and his army—just as God had warned.

Thankfully, God also promised that Judah would one day be restored through the Messiah. The book of Jeremiah shows that God's warnings and promises are true.

VITAL STATS/OUTLINE

The book of Jeremiah is not in chronological order. It describes true events, but not in the order that they happened.

A. Prophecies against Judah and Israel *(1–20)*

Jeremiah describes his call and then gives several oracles or visions threatening captivity for sinful nations.

B. Historical sections *(21–45)*

The decline and fall of Jerusalem.

C. Prophecies against other nations *(46–51)*

Egypt, Philistia, Moab, Ammon, Edom, Damascus, Elam, and Babylon.

D. Taken away to Babylonia *(52)*

The people are taken away from their homes. This is a punishment for their idolatry.

FAQs

Q: What made Jeremiah so brave?

A: God spoke to Jeremiah and told him he had set him apart for the special task of prophet. The Lord told Jeremiah not to be afraid. God promised to be with Jeremiah and to protect him.

Q: Didn't anyone listen to Jeremiah in 40 years?

A: The book mentions Baruch, who was

Jeremiah

Jeremiah's scribe, or secretary, and some palace officials who warned the king not to burn the scroll. Ebed-melech, another official, spoke up for Jeremiah when others wanted to kill him. There were probably some individuals among the people who are not named. But as a whole, the people did not listen.

LOOKOUT FOR . . .

As you read through Jeremiah, be on the lookout for . . .

Sins. Jeremiah is so sad about the sin of his nation that he talks about it many times.

Jerusalem. The book has two accounts of the fall of Jerusalem.

Forgiveness. While Jeremiah does speak about sin a lot, he also speaks about God's forgiveness when we repent.

SPECIAL

REPORT

Potters and pottery. Jeremiah 18 has a famous passage that compares God to a potter and people to clay. Potters were some of the first manufacturers in Jerusalem. They found their own clay, removed all the rocks from it, and

then placed it on wheels made of wood. After the pottery was the right shape, they would bake it so it became hard.

If the pottery became unsightly during the shaping process, the potters would simply smash it down and shape it over again. If the pottery broke after it was baked, the pieces were thrown into a potter's field *(Matthew 27:7,10)*.

STUDY QUESTIONS

• What did God say are the important things in life? *(Jeremiah 9:23-24)*

• What happened to Jeremiah and his friend Ebed-melech when Nebuchadnezzar captured Jerusalem? *(Jeremiah 39)*

LAMENTATIONS

WHY THIS BOOK?

Jeremiah was right, but he was not glad about it. He told the king of Judah and the people that God would punish them for their sins. God did what he said. God sent the Babylonians to destroy the city of Jerusalem. They captured the people and took them away to Babylonia.

But Jeremiah was not happy to be right. He was very sad. So he wrote the book of Lamentations.

Lamentations is a funeral dirge, or song. It tells about all the bad things that happened to Jerusalem and the people. It describes God's anger at the sin of Judah. Jeremiah speaks of his sorrow and tears for his people. He had warned them and he had wanted them to turn to God. But they did not repent, and they paid the price.

But in the middle of all the sadness, Jeremiah wrote of the hope people can have in the Lord. Jeremiah's lamentation also assures us that God does not give up on his people. God draws people back to himself.

VITAL STATS/OUTLINE

A. The desolation of Zion (1)

Jerusalem, which used to be a beautiful and powerful city, is now weak and gets taken over by another government.

B. God's anger against the people of Jerusalem (2)

God is finally going to punish the Israelites for their wickedness.

C. Jeremiah's grief (3)

Jeremiah tells God how sad he is. Then Jeremiah remembers God's faithfulness.

D. Confession and prayers for mercy (4–5)

Jeremiah prays that his people will be restored.

FAQs

Q: Why didn't Jeremiah tell the Israelites, "I told you so!"?

A: Jeremiah loved his people and the city of Jerusalem. He loved God, too. He wanted the people to love God and enjoy his blessings. He was truly sorry that they disobeyed and suffered for it.

Q: Why did Jeremiah cry?

A: Jeremiah cried because terrible things happened to his people. Their homes were ruined. Families were broken up. People were killed. Others were taken away to a foreign country. The city and the Temple were destroyed. Jeremiah had many reasons to cry.

LOOKOUT FOR . . .

As you read through Lamentations, be on the lookout for . . .

Sadness. Jeremiah is very sad about the sins of his people.

Prayers. Jeremiah suddenly breaks into prayer in many places in the midst of this story of Jerusalem's downfall.

Consequences. In Lamentations, the people of Israel are receiving the consequences of their sin.

SPECIAL REPORT

Jerusalem. Jerusalem was a walled city. During the time of Jeremiah the walls of a city could be six to nine meters thick, so it was no small thing that the walls of Jerusalem had been torn down or that they were rebuilt by Nehemiah at one time. The present walls

extend for four kilometers and have an average height of 12 meters.

There were gates built into the walls. Jerusalem has eight gates now, but they are not always in use. In Jeremiah's day, these gates could be closed at night or at times of danger.

Jerusalem was also the capital of Judah and the home of the Temple built by King Solomon. Jerusalem was where the death, resurrection, and ascension of Jesus took place. It was the most important city to the Jews. So when Jeremiah wept over Jerusalem, he was weeping for the whole nation.

STUDY QUESTIONS

• What was it like for the people when Jerusalem was destroyed? (Lamentations 2:11-12)

• What words of hope did Jeremiah have? (Lamentations 3:22-23, 31-33)

EZEKIEL

WHY THIS BOOK?

While Jeremiah spoke to the people in Jerusalem, Ezekiel spoke to the exiles in Babylonia. Ezekiel was younger than Jeremiah. The book of Ezekiel tells about Ezekiel's ministry and message to the exiles.

Ezekiel had been taken captive along with King Jehoiachin. God used Ezekiel as a living object lesson to show the exiles what would happen to them. For example, God told him to lay on his side for 390 days, "one day for each year of [the Israelites'] sins" (4:5). With living examples like this, Ezekiel delivered God's messages to his people.

Ezekiel emphasized that God was right to punish the Israelites for their sin and disobedience because they were so wicked. He also gave great hope to the people. God gave Ezekiel a vision of a valley full of dry bones that became live people. It was a promise that the nation of Israel would be fully restored. God promised to take away their "heart of stone" and give them a "heart of flesh."

VITAL STATS/OUTLINE

A. Warnings to Israel (1–24)

Ezekiel is called to be a prophet and begins to warn the Jews that God will punish their sin. He prophesies that Babylon will attack Jerusalem, and it happens just as he said it would.

B. Warnings to Israel's neighboring nations (25–32)

Ezekiel gives individual messages for the nations around Judah because they have treated God's people badly.

C. Visions of the future (33–48)

Ezekiel has an experience with bones coming back to life and begins to prophesy about the restoration of God's people.

121

FAQs

Q: Who were some of the other prophets to Israel at this time?

A: Jeremiah, Daniel, and Habakkuk were prophets of God at the same time as Ezekiel. Sometimes it may seem that believers are alone, but God always has many people who love and obey him.

Q: Why was God so angry at the Israelites?

A: The people God had chosen were acting as bad as the pagans around them. They were worshiping idols, sacrificing their children to false gods, robbing the poor, murdering, commiting sexual sins—completely turning their backs on the Lord.

Q: Why did God have Ezekiel be a living object lesson to the exiles?

A: Ezekiel's strange actions caused the people to pay attention to what Ezekiel was doing. It made it easier for him to explain God's message.

LOOKOUT FOR . . .

As you read through Ezekiel, be on the lookout for . . .

Prophecy of the future. Ezekiel prophesies many things that have already come true, and many that are still going to happen.

Calls to repentance. Ezekiel calls his own people as well as foreigners to repentance.

Visions. Ezekiel has several visions that teach him and help him understand what God wants to do.

SPECIAL REPORT

Egypt. The book of Ezekiel mentions Egypt many times. Egypt was and is a country to the southwest of Israel. It is the place that held Israel captive during Israel's infancy as a nation. Moses led the people of Israel out of slavery in Egypt.

The Nile is a famous river in Egypt. It is so important to that dry, desert country that in the past the people worshiped the river. There are also a lot of famous sights in Egypt such as the great pyramids and the sphinx.

The Israelites sometimes called Egypt "Mizraim." God's people both respected and feared the Egyptians. On several occasions Egypt was a place of safety for people of Israel. When Jacob's son Joseph came to Egypt he eventually was able to save the lives of his whole family through his work there. And when Jesus was born, Mary's husband Joseph took the family to Egypt to escape Herod.

STUDY QUESTIONS

   • What did God want Israel to do? *(Ezekiel 18:30-32)*
   • Why is it a good idea for us to listen to God and do what he says? *(Ezekiel 18:30-32)*

DANIEL

WHY THIS BOOK?

Imagine being kidnapped and taken to a foreign country. Imagine having your name changed and being given strange food to eat. Imagine seeing idols all around and people worshiping them.

That is what happened to Daniel and his three friends Shadrach, Meshach, and Abednego. They were young nobles from Jerusalem. Nebuchadnezzar wanted them to be trained to serve him. The book of Daniel records God's faithfulness to these young men who trusted God even in a strange land.

The book of Daniel shows how God was in control even when it seemed as if the king of Babylon was in control. God gave Daniel wisdom to know what the king had dreamed and how to interpret the dream. God also helped Shadrach, Meshach, and Abednego be brave and say no when the king demanded that they worship an idol.

Daniel

God did a miracle and saved them all. The book of Daniel shows that God was in control and had different jobs for each of them.

The second half of the book of Daniel is filled with prophecies about the future. These also show that God is in control.

VITAL STATS/OUTLINE

A. Stories of Daniel's life (1–6)
Daniel and his friends gain the king's trust. Daniel becomes known as a wise man. His friends are saved from the fiery furnace, and Daniel is saved from the lion's den.

B. Prophecy of the future (7–8)
Daniel has visions of a ram, a goat, and four beasts.

C. Prophecy of the coming Messiah (9)
Daniel prays for his people and prophesies about Jesus.

D. Prophecy of the end times (10–12)
Daniel describes visions and details about the end of the world.

FAQs

Q: Why were Daniel and his friends chosen to be trained for the king?

A: These young noblemen were handsome, intelligent, quick learners, and in excellent health. They were the kind of people the king wanted around him.

Q: Why did Nebuchadnezzar have Daniel and his friends' names changed?

A: The Hebrews' names gave praise to the Lord. Their Babylonian names honored Babylonian gods. Nebuchadnezzar may have been trying to change their loyalty from the true God to the Babylonian gods.

Q: What did Daniel do every day that got him thrown into the lions' den?

A: Daniel prayed three times every day. The king's officials knew that and tricked the king into making an unchangeable law. The law said no one could ask for anything from anyone except the king for 30 days. Daniel, however, continued his daily practice of praying to the Lord.

Daniel

LOOKOUT FOR . . .

As you read through Daniel, be on the lookout for . . .

Determination and decisions. Daniel determines in his heart when he is young that he is going to live the kind of life God wants him to. Each time he makes a decision it is a decision to follow God's way of doing things.

Prophecy. Daniel explains the king's dreams and tells him about the future. Daniel also describes things that will happen in our future.

Kings. The book of Daniel mentions several different kings. That is because while Babylon is holding the Israelites captive, the government keeps getting new leadership.

SPECIAL REPORT

Furnace. The furnace that Daniel's friends were thrown into was not meant for people. It was actually the kind of furnace that is used for other purposes. At that time furnaces could be used for smelting metals such as copper, tin, iron, or lead. Some could also be used for making bricks or pottery. Such furnaces were sometimes called "kilns." Other kinds of furnaces were used for baking bread. Sometimes the word for "furnace" was also translated "oven."

It was the Persians who had the idea of using this hot, fiery place for executions. Many furnaces had a hole at the top to throw in materials and a door at the bottom on the side to pull out the metals, bricks, or breads. The fire was especially hot in the furnace the day Daniel's friends were thrown in. Even the

guards were burned to death when they came near. It was truly a miracle that God could protect those men in the fiery furnace.

STUDY QUESTIONS

• What decree did King Darius make when he saw that the Lord protected Daniel from the hungry lions? *(Daniel 6:25-27)*

• How did Daniel describe the judgment of the nations? *(Daniel 7:9-10)*

HOSEA

WHY THIS BOOK?

It is very sad when husbands and wives get divorced. The husband, the wife, and the children all suffer. That is just one reason God wants families to try to stay together.

In the book of Hosea, God compares Israel (the northern kingdom) to a wife. His message to Israel is that he loves her and wants her to stay. But she is interested in other men.

The prophet Hosea went through the same sorrow God was going through. Hosea married a woman named Gomer, but Gomer left him for other men. Even some of her children were fathered by other men. But God told Hosea to bring her home and keep on loving her. Hosea's love for Gomer was like God's love for his people.

The people of Israel were unfaithful to God. They trusted in military help from Assyria and Egypt. They worshiped the false god Baal and mixed idol worship with worship of the Lord. They were rich, but they were not loyal to God. It broke his heart. God sent Hosea to urge them to come back to him.

VITAL STATS/OUTLINE

A. Hosea's unhappy marriage *(1–3)*

Even though Hosea's wife is unfaithful to him, he continues to take care of her.

B. Israel's sin *(4–7)*

Hosea describes the sin of Israel by accusing them of worshiping other gods and not trusting the one true God to take care of them.

C. Judgment is coming *(8–10)*

There will be consequences for Israel's disobedience.

D. God is faithful *(11–14)*

Hosea reminds the people of Israel that God loves them and is kind to those who love him back.

FAQs

Q: Why did God tell Hosea to marry an unfaithful wife?

A: God wanted his people to see his love as they watched Hosea. The people could see how unfaithful Gomer was and how much Hosea loved her. They did not understand that they were just as unfaithful to God as Gomer was to Hosea. Hosea and Gomer were an object lesson to God's people.

Hosea

Q: What kinds of things were the people of Israel doing that caused God to punish them?

A: The people forgot God and his ways. They were worshiping idols. They were lying, stealing, cursing, murdering, committing adultery, and doing all kinds of violence all over the land.

LOOKOUT FOR . . .

As you read through Hosea, be on the lookout for . . .

Meanings of names. Hosea chooses the names of his children for a reason. Notice what the names mean.

Israel and Judah. When Hosea was prophesying, the kingdom of the Hebrews was divided into Judah and Israel. Hosea addressed them together at times and separately at other times.

God's love. The book of Hosea includes beautiful words of love from God to his people.

SPECIAL REPORT

Jezreel. Jezreel is a city on the border of the land given to

Issachar. The first son of Hosea and Gomer was named for this city.

It was in Jezreel that the evil king Ahab built his palace. It was there that Ahab had a man named Naboth killed just so Ahab could get his vineyard. It was there that Ahab met with Elijah and it was there that evil Queen Jezebel met her death. It was at the gates of Jezreel that the heads of seventy sons of Ahab were placed after the sons were executed by King Jehu.

From this city there was an excellent view of the plain reaching toward Jordan. This plain is called the Valley of Jezreel.

STUDY QUESTIONS

• What did Hosea say when he asked Israel to repent? *(Hosea 14:1-3)*

• What did God promise to do if the people repented? *(Hosea 14:4-8)*

JOEL

WHY THIS BOOK?

How many locusts would it take to block out the sun like a dark rain cloud? That's how many the prophet Joel predicted would attack the crops of Judah. In the book of Joel the prophet tried to wake up the people of Judah from their sin. He told them that God was going to send such a large plague of locusts that nothing would remain. Every bit of vegetation would be eaten by bugs. There would be no food.

Some people wonder if Joel was speaking of actual locusts. They think he might have been predicting a mighty army destroying everything. Whichever he was talking about, the destruction would be terrible. Joel urged the southern kingdom of Judah to repent and turn to God.

Judah was prosperous at the time of Joel. But instead of being thankful to God, the people became self-centered. They turned to idolatry and sin. They thought everything was just fine. Why worry?

Joel warned of "the day of the Lord," a time still in the future when God will judge everyone and put everything right. But even though God is the all-powerful Judge, he still is merciful. He wants people to repent and turn to him. He wants to bless those who trust him.

VITAL STATS/OUTLINE

A. The locust plague *(1:1–2:18)*

Joel predicts a plague of locusts (grasshoppers) and an enemy invasion.

B. Future blessings and judgments *(2:19–3:21)*

Joel predicts the end of the world when God redeems his people and restores Israel.

FAQs

Q: Why did Joel talk about locusts?

A: Locusts travel in swarms and eat all the plants and crops in their path. They can completely wipe out an entire field of crops in hours. To say that God's judgment would be like a storm of locusts would scare anybody who knew how bad a locust swarm can be. God wanted this terrible message to shock the people into listening to him!

Q: What does it mean to "turn to God?"

A: Turning to God does not mean just going to church or believing that God exists. God wants people to truly be sorry for their sin and stop doing it. He wants people to ask his forgiveness. Spending time talking with him and reading his Word to know his will is important.

LOOKOUT FOR . . .

As you read through Joel, be on the lookout for . . .

A plague. God often uses extreme natural events to get the attention of the people of God.

End times. Joel describes many things that will happen when Jesus comes back and rules the world.

SPECIAL REPORT

Locusts. Locusts are a kind of grasshopper. They fly in swarms and can destroy large amounts of crops or green plants in a short amount of time. In the Bible, locusts are also referred to as "devourers," "pests." and "katydids." While locusts can eat a lot, they can also be eaten themselves, as it says in *Leviticus 11:21-22*. John the Baptist ate locusts and wild honey (*see Mark 1:6*).

God used locusts as a judgment once before. When Moses was freeing the Israelites from Egypt one of the ten plagues was a plague of locusts (*Exodus 10:4*). The prophet Joel describes a devastating plague of locusts that will come as a punishment for Israel's sin (*Joel 1:2-4*). These descriptions do not compare, though, with the prediction in

Revelation 9:3-10. The locusts there are described as a great army with the ability to destroy everything in their path.

STUDY QUESTIONS

- What was the army of locusts like? *(Joel 2:1-11)*
- What promise did the Lord give to everyone? *(Joel 2:32)*

AMOS

WHY THIS BOOK?

A farmer speaking to city people might feel uneasy telling them about their sin, but not Amos. Amos was a shepherd from the southern kingdom. God sent him to warn the Israelites in the northern kingdom. The book of Amos is the record of Amos' message.

Amos started out warning the surrounding nations for their constant sinning. Then he spoke against the people of Judah. Perhaps the people of Israel cheered him on. But then he spoke against Israel too. Everyone would have to answer to God. That was a different story!

Amaziah the high priest opposed Amos and reported him to King Jeroboam II. As you might expect, Amos' message was not popular.

Amos spoke against the Israelites for their attitude. They were wealthy and happy. That's all that mattered to them. They neglected the poor. They oppressed them. They sold them into slavery to buy luxuries for themselves.

The Israelites had a show of religion. But they worshiped idols and did not follow the Lord. Amos called them to repent.

About 28 years after Amos finished speaking to Israel, God kept his promise. The wealthy Israelites who sold their countrymen into slavery became slaves themselves. The Assyrians took them away to other lands.

VITAL STATS/OUTLINE

A. Judgment on foreign nations *(1–2)*

God calls Amos and announces Israel's punishment for their sin and corruption.

B. Judgment on Samaria *(3–6)*

Several prophecies, each beginning with the call for the people to listen.

C. Five visions and Bethel *(7–9)*

Five visions (bad news) and some closing promises (good news).

Amos

FAQs

Q: What did the nations around Israel do to deserve God's punishment?

A: They had mistreated God's people. Even though the people of Israel and Judah forgot God and sinned against him, they were God's chosen people. He never lets anyone get away with harming them.

Q: What was Amos' message to Israel?

A: Amos reminded the people of Israel of all that God had done to get their attention. God sent disaster, withheld water, and sent mildew on the gardens trying to get them to recognize his power. Instead they bragged about their wealth and did not depend on God.

Q: What kinds of bad things did the Israelites do?

A: They took bribes. They sold the poor into slavery. They pretended to worship God when they really did not mean it. They bragged about giving offerings to God. They cared more about things than about God or people.

LOOKOUT FOR . . .

As you read through Amos, be on the lookout for . . .

Messages from God. Amos says more than once, "Listen to what the Lord says . . ."

Visions. Some of Amos's visions include fire, a plumb line, ripe fruit, and God at an altar.

Charges. God charges his people with many specific sins.

SPECIAL REPORT

Plumb line. A plumb line is a cord or a string with a weight tied to the end. It is also called a "plummet." Plumb lines were used by masons and construction workers. They would hang up the string and let the weight at the bottom pull down on it. They would then use the string as a guide, to help them build a straight wall.

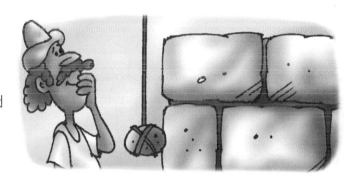

The plumb line was also used to inspect a wall to see if it had been built well. This is the use described in the vision in Amos 7:7-9. God said that he would hold a plumb line up to Israel. He explained though that this plumb line would measure righteousness. This would show him the sin there and he would correct that sin.

STUDY QUESTION

• How does God show his mercy even when he is angry at sin? (Amos 3:7)

OBADIAH

WHY THIS BOOK?

Brothers should help each other, especially when one is being beat up by a bully. But the people of Edom did not help their brothers the Israelites.

The people of Edom were related to the people of Israel. They both had Abraham and Isaac as ancestors. The Edomites were descendants of Esau. The Israelites were descended from Esau's brother Jacob.

The book of Obadiah tells of God's judgment on the people of Edom. They did not help their Israelite relatives in Judah. When the Babylonians attacked Jerusalem, the Edomites cheered them on. They actually helped the Babylonians capture the people of Judah! Then they plundered Jerusalem and took what was left behind. The Edomites were also proud and thought nothing could hurt them.

Obadiah is the shortest book in the Old Testament, but it tells an important message. God takes care of his people, and he punishes those who hurt them.

VITAL STATS/OUTLINE

A. Judgment on Edom *(1:1-16)*

Through Obadiah's vision God claims judgment on Edom for causing harm to Israel and rejoicing in that harm.

B. Israel will be restored *(1:17-21)*

Describes a time when Israel will have great power over Edom.

FAQs

Q: Where did the Edomites live?

A: The Edomites lived south of Judah. They shared a boundary and were close enough to help the Israelites.

Q: Why were the Edomites so proud?

A: That was their way. Also, the people of Edom had carved a city out of the rocks. They were up high in a fortress that seemed safe and secure. They were very proud of themselves and thought they were safe.

Q: What judgment did God actually send on Edom?

A: The nation of Edom was completely destroyed.

LOOKOUT FOR . . .

As you read through Obadiah, be on the lookout for . . .
Reasons for God's judgment. Obadiah lists some specifics that

God holds Edom accountable for.

Signs of Israel's restoration. Notice how God describes the shift in power when Israel gets the upper hand over Edom.

SPECIAL REPORT

Edom. The people of Edom were descended from Esau. Their country was also called Seir or Mount Seir. The land was between the Dead Sea and the Gulf of Aqabah. It was about 140 kilometers long and 25 kilometers wide.

When Esau came to this land he married the daughter of one of the Horites, or cave dwellers, who were already living there. As Esau's descendants grew, they eventually took over the land from the Horites. At one time, King David conquered the Edomites and had control of the whole country. During the reign of later kings Edom won its independence again.

Esau and his twin brother Jacob (whose descendants are the Israelites) were often enemies of each other. It is no wonder, then, that their descendants would mistreat each other and would need God's intervention.

STUDY QUESTION

• What prophecy did Obadiah make about Israel and Edom? *(Obadiah 1:17-18)*

JONAH

WHY THIS BOOK?

The Hebrew people had a hard time learning that God wanted them to obey. But after they learned that lesson, it was difficult to learn that God still loved people of other nations. The book of Jonah tells about Jonah's struggle with God's love for others. This is the only book of prophecy that tells more about the prophet than the prophet's message.

Jonah was the first Hebrew prophet sent as a missionary to a pagan country. He was a prophet to the northern kingdom of Israel. Then God sent him to Nineveh. Nineveh was the capital of the great Assyrian empire at a time when it was very strong.

The Assyrians were not lovable people. They were fierce warriors and cruel captors. When God told Jonah to go to Nineveh to preach to the people there, Jonah went in the opposite direction.

Jonah tried to go as far away as possible. But even in a ship in the middle of the Mediterranean Sea, Jonah could not hide from God. After suffering for his disobedience, Jonah finally repented and obeyed the Lord's command.

Jonah learned that God's salvation is for all who will repent and believe.

VITAL STATS/OUTLINE

A. Jonah's call and his escape *(1)*

God asks Jonah to go to Nineveh, but Jonah runs the other way. During a storm, Jonah is thrown overboard from a boat and rescued by a large fish.

B. Jonah's prayer *(2)*

Jonah thanks and praises God for saving him.

C. Preaching to Nineveh *(3)*

After the fish spits Jonah out on shore, the prophet obeys God and preaches to Nineveh.

D. Jonah is disappointed (4)

The people of Nineveh repent, and Jonah is disappointed that God does not punish them for their sins.

FAQs

Q: Why didn't Jonah want to preach to the people of Nineveh?

A: The people of Nineveh were enemies of Israel and very cruel. Jonah hated them. Jonah also knew that God is merciful and kind. He did not want the people of Nineveh to repent because he knew God would forgive them if they did. He wanted them to be punished for their wickedness.

Q: How did Jonah get swallowed by a fish?

A: God sent the fish to rescue Jonah from drowning in the sea. In fact, God sent the fish in answer to Jonah's prayer for help. Jonah tells about it in chapter 2. The fish took Jonah to shore all the way from the middle of the open sea.

LOOKOUT FOR . . .

As you read through Jonah, be on the lookout for . . .

Jonah's pride. It shows up more than once.

Jonah's prayers. Jonah is honest with God in his prayers, even when he is angry.

SPECIAL REPORT

Nineveh. Nineveh was one of the most ancient cities of the world. It was founded on the banks of the Tigris River by Nimrod, Noah's great-grandson. For many years it was the capital of the Assyrian empire and was an important city from King David's reign until Manasseh's reign.

Nineveh was ruled by kings except for a span of about fifty years around 800 B.C. We do not know what happened to cause that lapse between kings, but it was probably within that time that Jonah went to Nineveh and saw them repent of their sin. God gave them many more years because of that repentance.

Nineveh was destroyed around 612 B.C., about 2,609 years ago, by the Assyrians. This was just after Nahum's prophecy against the city.

STUDY QUESTIONS

• What was it like for Jonah in the sea and inside the fish? (Jonah 2:1-9)

• What happened when Jonah preached to the people of Nineveh? (Jonah 3:1-10)

• Why did Jonah become angry? (Jonah 4:1-4)

MICAH

WHY THIS BOOK?

It is not enough for people to worship God and then forget what God teaches them to do. God expects people who love him to be kind and merciful to others. He wants them to do good. And he wants them to worship him sincerely.

The prophet Micah explained this message in the book of Micah. He told about God's coming judgment on Samaria (in Israel) and on Jerusalem (in Judah) for disobeying God. But Micah also told of the hope and peace that Messiah would bring. Hundreds of years before Jesus was born, Micah predicted that Messiah would be born in Bethlehem. It was this prediction that the wise men followed. They asked Herod at Jerusalem where the new king was. The priests told them in Bethlehem.

Micah was a prophet the same time as Isaiah and Hosea. His book is written in Hebrew poetry. His message of judgment was against those who stole, lied, oppressed the poor, murdered, craved money, and pretended to worship the Lord. Assyria overran Israel during Micah's ministry. Micah also predicted that Judah would fall. But Messiah would be the new king, a righteous, good king.

VITAL STATS/OUTLINE

A. Oppression and false prophets *(1-3)*

Micah speaks directly to Samaria and Jerusalem (the two Hebrew capitals) about the sin of the people and of the leadership.

B. Christ's coming kingdom *(4-5)*

Micah predicts Jesus' birth and eternal reign.

C. God judges and forgives *(6-7)*

Micah states God's case against Israel as well as Israel's hope of God's forgiveness.

FAQs

Q: Why would God punish Israel and Judah?

A: The people were ignoring God's commands to treat each other with respect. They were taking property from widows and other poor people. The false prophets were saying that everything was fine. God wanted them to know that these issues were important.

Q: But doesn't God love his people? How could he hurt them?

A: It is because God loves people that he punishes sin. He wants people to repent and turn to him. Sometimes when people are enjoying God's blessings, they forget him. He has to get their attention. Sometimes he does that with trouble.

Q: How did the priests pretend to be worshiping God?

A: The priests would carry out the ceremonies of worship. But they did not mean it. In their hearts they were scheming to get wealth and power.

LOOKOUT FOR . . .

As you read through Micah, be on the lookout for . . .

The Messiah. Micah tells about Christ's coming long before it happens. He even names the town of Christ's birth.

Advice. Micah gives great advice on how to follow God in our everyday lives.

Samaria. Micah talks a lot about the punishment that the people of Samaria will receive for their sins.

SPECIAL REPORT

Samaria. The term "Samaria" can refer to a city, a region, or a country. When the Israelite kingdom split into the northern and southern kingdoms, the northern kingdom built Samaria as its capital. The land where they built the city was bought from a man named Shemer, and it is

from that word that the city got its name. The northern kingdom was made up of ten tribes of Israelites. Sometimes people refer to Samaria as the whole region of land held by those ten tribes as well as the capital city.

Micah prophesied to both the city of Samaria (capital of the northern kingdom) and the city of Jerusalem (capital of the southern kingdom). Both cities were filled with Israelites who had disobeyed and forgotten the one true God.

Samaria was built on a hill. It had a wall (as most cities did at that time) all the way around it and gates that could be closed at night and during an attack. Samaria stood through many battles, and its ruins are still there today.

STUDY QUESTIONS

• What prophecy of Micah's came true in Bethlehem? (Micah 5:2-5; Matthew 2:1-6)

• How does Micah describe God? (Micah 7:18-20)

NAHUM

WHY THIS BOOK?

Some nations are so powerful it seems they could never be defeated. That is how it was with Assyria. Assyria had a large, powerful, fierce army. They had strong chariots with sharp knives sticking out of the wheel hubs. The soldiers were not afraid of anyone. They killed more people than could be counted. They plundered nation after nation. They had no sense of right and wrong. It did not bother them to be cruel and vicious to their captives.

At one time they repented, when Jonah preached to them. But by the time Nahum became a prophet about 100 years later, they were just as wicked as before.

Nahum's book is God's message to Nineveh, the great capital of Assyria. The news is not good. God's patience with Nineveh had run out. The Assyrians had taken Israel captive. Now the righteous Judge was going to destroy wicked Assyria. Nothing could be worse than to have God be against you!

But there is good news in the book of Nahum. God promised the people of Judah that Assyria would never harm Judah again.

VITAL STATS/OUTLINE

A. God's nature (1)
God's anger, patience, and power.
B. Nineveh's destruction (2–3)
Nahum describes the destruction of Nineveh and God's reasons for destroying them.

FAQs

Q: If the people of Nineveh repented when Jonah preached to them, why were they wicked again?

A: Each generation of people has to choose whether to follow God. Parents' decisions can influence their children. The children will benefit from parents' good decisions. But the children have to decide to believe and obey God too.

Q: How did God destroy Assyria?

A: God used other nations to destroy Assyria. In 612 B.C. he used the Babylonians and the Medes to fight Assyria. They did to Assyria what it had done so many times to other nations. They waged war against the people and pillaged the wealth. The city of Nineveh was so completely destroyed that no one could identify its ruins until 1845—more than 2,000 years afterward!

LOOKOUT FOR . . .

As you read through Nahum, be on the lookout for . . .

Traits of God. Even though this is a prophecy against Assyria, the book tells a lot about God.

Punishment. Nahum makes it clear that the people of Assyria will receive harsh punishment for their sin.

SPECIAL REPORT

Assyria. Assyria was right beside Babylonia. They were fighting all the time and moving their border back and forth. Israel was beside both of these empires so Israel often had to fight them and eventually was taken over by both of them for a time.

Assyria's capital was Nineveh.

Assyria was probably started by a colony of Babylonians. Because of that their cultures were a lot alike and their religions were too. The Assyrians honored the false god Asshur as their founder. Some of their other gods were Anu, Bel, Ea, Shamash, and Ishtar. While the Assyrians battled the Babylonians, they also had times where they worked together and almost got control of the world as it was then.

STUDY QUESTION

• Why do some people say God is angry all the time, while other people say he is loving? *(Nahum 1:7-8)*

HABAKKUK

WHY THIS BOOK?

It is not much fun watching the news or reading the newspaper these days. People steal, lie, cheat, beat up others, kill their enemies—and their friends—and do many other wicked things.

Believe it or not, it is not any different from when the prophet Habakkuk lived in Judah more than 2,500 years ago! Habakkuk had the same questions many people have today. He asked God how come he was not doing anything about all that evil. Habakkuk knew that God is just and holy. He could not figure out how God could let all the bad people get away with doing bad things.

Habakkuk did the right thing with his questions. He went to God with them. God answered him and gave him a message that people can still read today.

The surprising thing was that God had a plan that was stranger than anything Habakkuk could imagine. God was going to use the Babylonians to punish the people of Judah.

This made more questions for Habakkuk. The Babylonians were far more wicked than the people of Judah. How could God use them to punish his people? The Babylonians were proud. They did not know that God was using them to turn his people back to him. The Babylonians' sins would be their undoing.

God assured Habakkuk that someday he will punish all those who are against God. But those who trust in God will have true life ("the righteous will live by their faith," 2:4).

VITAL STATS/OUTLINE

A. Habakkuk's burden (1–2)
Habakkuk asks questions, and God gives his replies.

B. Habakkuk's prayer (3)
Habakkuk admits God's greatness and sings this prayer to honor him.

FAQs

Q: What did God do when Habakkuk asked hard questions?

A: God did not get angry at Habakkuk. He answered his questions and explained

that justice would be done. God said there was an appointed time, and he told Habakkuk to be patient and wait for it.

Q: What did Habakkuk do with God's answers?

A: At first Habakkuk was more confused. Then he saw that God is in control. He asked God to have mercy on Judah in the time of discipline. Then he praised God.

LOOKOUT FOR . . .

As you read through Habakkuk, be on the lookout for . . .
Questions. Habakkuk asks God some hard questions.
Answers. God answers Habakkuk's questions.
Praises. Habakkuk praises God for his greatness.

SPECIAL REPORT

Babylonia. Babylonia was a powerful kingdom that was known for many things, especially two famous cities. The capital city of Babylonia was Babylon, which is mentioned in both the New and Old Testaments. Another important Babylonian city was Ur. It was from this city that Abraham came.

Babylonia is famous for its unique style of pottery, the beginnings of writing called "cuneiform," the oldest ziggurat or tall tower at that time, and a special style of weaving (see *Joshua 7:21*). Because the country was so large and so close to the Hebrew nation, it was a constant threat. (Countries at that time were trying to broaden their borders and take over other countries.)

STUDY QUESTIONS

- What promises did God give to Habakkuk? *(Habakkuk 2:14, 20)*
- How did Habakkuk praise God? *(Habakkuk 3:1-19)*
- What did Habakkuk promise God? *(Habakkuk 3:17-18)*

ZEPHANIAH

WHY THIS BOOK?

God had sent many prophets to warn the people of Judah that judgment was coming. The book of Zephaniah was one of the last ones written before the Jews were exiled to Babylon.

Zephaniah prophesied during the reign of King Josiah of Judah. He also served when Jeremiah first started giving God's messages to the people of Jerusalem. King Josiah was the last good king of Judah. He worked hard to lead the people away from idols back to the Lord. Zephaniah probably helped Josiah understand God's word and how to apply it to his people.

Manasseh and Amon, two kings before Josiah, had led the people far from God. They worshiped idols such as Baal, Molech, and others. Worshiping Molech included sacrificing children! God hated this practice. The people thought they could worship the true God and the idols.

The day of the Lord that Zephaniah predicted had two meanings. The first was the Babylonian exile. The second will be on the final day of judgment. On that day, God will punish all who have rejected him. Those who trust in him will live with him in heaven.

God is patiently giving people time to turn to him. Then there will be joy and blessing.

VITAL STATS/OUTLINE

A. Coming judgment for Judah *(1–2:4)*
Zephaniah tells about the coming destruction of Jerusalem.
B. Coming judgment for all nations *(2:4-15)*
Zephaniah tells about the time when God will judge the whole world.
C. Jerusalem's rebellion and redemption *(3)*
God will one day purify his people.

FAQs

Q: If Josiah and Zephaniah helped the people turn back to God, why did God still punish them?

A: Josiah had a true desire to please God, but most of the people did not have a real change of heart. A few years after Josiah died, the people continued their sinful ways of life.

Q: How can Zephaniah's prophecy have two meanings?

A: Actually, several of the prophecies in the Old Testament work that way. The first meaning would come

about soon after the prophet spoke. The second meaning would come about later. Some of Zephaniah's prophecies tell of events that hold promise for the future.

LOOKOUT FOR . . .

As you read through Zephaniah, be on the lookout for . . .

Day of the Lord. Zephaniah talks about two days of the Lord. These are days when God intervenes in the world in a big way. One of those days will be in the end of the world as we know it.

Joy. Even though Zephaniah is talking about punishment, there is a lot of joy in the end of his message.

SPECIAL REPORT

Moab and Ammon. The countries of Moab and Ammon were named for the families that settled there. The families were named for their most important ancestor. Moab was the son of Lot's oldest daughter. Ammon was the son of Lot's youngest daughter.

Lot was Abraham's nephew. He got involved with two very sinful cities, Sodom and Gomorrah. After he left those cities his daughters each had a son. The names of these sons

were Moab and Ammon. When Moab and Ammon grew up they moved away from Lot, and their families settled in these lands that were then named after them. After many years the people of Israel (Abraham's descendants) came back to settle their land, and the people of Moab and Ammon (descendants of Moab and Ammon) fought against them. This is a shame because Abraham was so kind to Lot.

Zephaniah prophesied against Moab and Ammon because they fought Israel, because they tried to take land that was not theirs, and because they tried to tempt Israel into being unfaithful to God.

STUDY QUESTION

• What good promise did God make to Israel? (Zephaniah 3:14-20)

HAGGAI

WHY THIS BOOK?

"First things first" is an expression that means the most important things should be done first. Soon after King Cyrus defeated the Babylonians, he let the Jews return to Jerusalem to rebuild the Temple. The returned exiles started the job, but enemies threatened and discouraged them. For as long as 10 years they stopped working on the Temple.

God sent the prophet Haggai to get the people to finish the job. Haggai's messages are recorded in the book of Haggai. Haggai and Zechariah worked along with Ezra and Nehemiah to help the Jews.

The people were building their own homes and leaving God's Temple in ruins. Haggai said that that was not right. The prophet reminded them that they needed to finish the Temple. Meanwhile, they were working hard but had little to show for it. Haggai said that was because the Lord was working against them. He was not blessing

their efforts, and they never felt satisfied.

Haggai said the people should put first things first; they should rebuild God's Temple. They should care about spiritual matters, and God would satisfy their needs and their hearts.

VITAL STATS/OUTLINE

A. Rebuilding the Temple *(1:1–2:9)*

Haggai encourages the people to rebuild the Temple now and stop putting it off.

B. Promises *(2:10-23)*

God promises to meet the people's needs if they will finish their work on the Temple.

FAQs

Q: What were the people doing in Jerusalem all those years?

A: They settled down to live and build their homes. Some of them lived in fancy houses or were working on them. They grew lots of grain, grapes, and olive trees. But they were not building the Temple, so their hard work did not go very far.

Q: What did the people do after Haggai spoke to them?

A: The leaders and the people responded quickly and followed Haggai's advice. Within a few weeks they got serious about rebuilding the Temple.

Haggai

Q: After the people obeyed, what did God do?

A: As soon as the people started to work on the Temple, God said he would bless them and make their crops grow.

LOOKOUT FOR . . .

As you read through Haggai, be on the lookout for . . .

Dates. This book actually gives us the dates of Haggai's messages.

Inspiration. Haggai was like a cheerleader, cheering on God's people to work on the Temple.

Results. The people responded to Haggai's words and rebuilt the Temple.

SPECIAL REPORT

The Temple. Solomon built the first Temple with the finest of building materials. But each time the Israelites would fall away from God, they would stop taking care of it. And each time their enemies

fought them, their enemies would try to destroy it. This is why we read so much in the Old Testament about the Temple being rebuilt.

During the time of Haggai, the Temple had been completely destroyed. The Israelites did not have much money or many resources to build a beautiful Temple again. But they tried. Zerubbabel was the governor. He was in charge of the city. Joshua was the religious ruler. Together they led the people to rebuild the Temple. It was not as fine as Solomon's Temple, but it reminded the people that worshiping God was important.

STUDY QUESTIONS

• How did God encourage his people? *(I Iaggai 2:4-5)*

• What did God say to the people as soon as they started to work? *(Haggai 2:18-19)*

ZECHARIAH

WHY THIS BOOK?

What would it be like to know the future? God gave the prophets messages about the future. Some of the messages were warnings of coming judgment if the people did not repent of sin and turn to God. Some messages gave hope of comfort and peace.

Zechariah was a prophet to the people who had returned to Jerusalem. He worked with the prophet Haggai to encourage them to continue building the Temple. His message told of God's anger and grace.

Of all the Old Testament books, the book of Zechariah is filled with the most prophecies about the Messiah. There are prophecies about his first coming to earth when he was crucified and rose again. There are prophecies about his second coming as the almighty King. There are many prophecies about the end of time.

People who read and study God's Word today can know something about what the future holds. God does not tell exact dates, but he warns people not to follow false prophets. He promises that at the end of time, those who reject God will be punished forever. Those who trust Jesus Christ the Messiah will enjoy his peace and everlasting life.

VITAL STATS/OUTLINE

A. Introduction and visions (1–6)

Zechariah tells about visions of horns, blacksmiths, olive trees, lampstands, and flying scrolls.

B. True worship (7–8)

Zechariah encourages his people to trust God and to repair the Temple.

C. The future of Israel (9–14)

Zechariah predicts that God will judge Israel's enemies, deliver Israel, and rule the earth.

FAQs

Q: How do we know that Jesus Christ is the Messiah that Zechariah was talking about?

A: Zechariah wrote his prophecies about 500 years before Jesus was born. Jesus' life fulfills the many details given in Zechariah's prophecies. Jesus is the only one who fits the description that

Zechariah gave.

    Q: What's so great about Jesus fulfilling the prophecies?

    A: Since God's Word is true concerning Jesus' first coming to earth, people can have confidence that his other promises are also true. God gives fair warning about judgment and comforting promises about blessing.

LOOKOUT FOR . . .

    As you read through Zechariah, be on the lookout for . . .

    Visions. Zechariah has eight visions or dreams.

    Prophecies. Zechariah gives many prophecies that came true in the life of Jesus.

SPECIAL REPORT

    Myrtle trees. In one of Zechariah's visions he sees a man (who was really an angel) standing among some myrtle trees. A myrtle is a small evergreen shrub. It has white flowers, blue berries, and leaves with a scent. The Jews thought this plant stood for peace and prosperity. It was an important plant to them. When the

Jews celebrated their Festival of Shelters (or Tabernacles) they used myrtle branches to cover the temporary shelters they lived in.

Zechariah thought of myrtles as a plant of peace. It must have been comforting to Zechariah to get good news from an angel who was surrounded by myrtles.

STUDY QUESTIONS

• What instructions did God tell the people they should do? (*Zechariah 8:16-17*)

• How does Zechariah's prophecy about the king compare with Jesus' fulfillment of the prophecy? (*Zechariah 9:9-10; Matthew 21:1-11*)

MALACHI

WHY THIS BOOK?

Malachi was the last of the prophets to Judah and Israel. The Temple had been rebuilt. The walls of Jerusalem had been completed. But the people were cutting corners in their worship of God. The priests were not doing the sacrifices properly. Men were divorcing their wives and marrying younger women who worshiped idols. The children were growing up believing in idols. And the people were not tithing their crops and animals to the Lord. That was a lot like stealing from God.

Malachi made it clear that God's people had to take their worship more seriously, and he promised blessing for those who did. His very last words were a promise of another prophet to help the people before judgment came. Malachi was the last of the prophets to Israel and Judah until the coming of Jesus. After Malachi, no prophet spoke for more than 400 years.

VITAL STATS/OUTLINE

A. Unworthy worship *(1:1–2:9)*
God confronts Israel's leaders about their sin.
B. A call to repentance *(2:10-17)*
Malachi reminds his people to trust God and to be faithful to him.
C. The coming judgment *(3–4)*
Malachi predicts a day of judgment and deliverance.

FAQs

Q: What was wrong with sacrificing a crippled animal?

A: God used the sacrifices as an object lesson to show the seriousness of sin and the need for forgiveness. God is holy and requires our best—not something sick or broken.

Q: How did the priests mess up the worship?

A: The priests were not showing respect to the Lord. They complained about the burden of having to make sacrifices. As the leaders they had a lot of influence on people's attitudes and actions. Also they were not teaching the truth.

Q: Why does God hate divorce?

A: God wants husbands and wives to love each other and to be faithful to each other. He knows that people, especially children, get hurt very badly when families break up. He wants families to be safe and happy places for kids to grow up.

Q: Who is the prophet like Elijah that God promised (Malachi 4:5)?

A: John the Baptist.

LOOKOUT FOR . . .

As you read through Malachi, be on the lookout for . . .

Questions and answers. Malachi uses questions and answers throughout his messages.

Priests. Many of Malachi's references to priests apply to church leaders today.

SPECIAL REPORT

Grapes. Often in the Old Testament when a prophet describes a time when things are going well, he will mention grapes. Sometimes he says that the grapes will bring much wine. Sometimes, as in Malachi, he says that the grapes will not wither (dry up).

Grapes are the

first plant to be recorded in biblical history (Genesis 9:20). They grow on climbing vines that can be left to grow wild or can be tended, or cultivated, in vineyards. For the Jews, grapes were a symbol of wealth and good fortune, and the grape harvest (the time they picked the grapes) was a time of celebration and rejoicing.

STUDY QUESTIONS

- How did the people make God tired? (Malachi 2:17)
- How will God treat those who trust him? (Malachi 3:16-18)
- Who is the prophet like Elijah whom God promised? (Malachi 4:5 6; Matthew 17:10-13)

THE NEW TESTAMENT

MATTHEW

WHY THIS BOOK?

Four hundred years is a long time to wait for a message from God. That is how long it was between the writing of the last book in the Old Testament (Malachi) and God's next message. After all those years of silence, God finally sent his Son, Jesus Christ.

The book of Matthew was written by one of Jesus' disciples. It is a good link between the Old Testament and the New Testament. It does not tell everything that Jesus did and said. But it shows that Jesus fulfills the prophecies about the Messiah, the King of the Jews.

Matthew includes Jesus' genealogy, the list of his ancestors. It goes back to Abraham to show that Jesus is the one God promised. Matthew makes it clear that Joseph was Mary's husband and that Mary was Jesus' mother, but that God was Jesus' father. Joseph was Jesus' legal or earthly father. This showed that Jesus was in the royal line of King David.

The book of Matthew is best known for Jesus' Sermon on the Mount (5–7) and the Great

Commission *(28:18-20)*. But there are other things in Matthew that mean a lot to Jewish people. They include the visit of the wise men, what Jesus said about the law, the Kingdom of Heaven, and Jesus' triumphal entry into Jerusalem.

Jesus came as King of the Jews. But the people did not recognize him because they thought he would set them free from the Romans. The Jews did not expect their king to be crucified. But Jesus rose from the dead, proving he is God's Son.

VITAL STATS/OUTLINE

The outline of Matthew is very interesting. It goes back and forth between Jesus' teaching or sermons and his miracles.

A. Jesus' birth *(1–2)*

Jesus is born in Bethlehem. The wise men come to worship him, but this puts Jesus in danger, so his parents take him to Egypt.

B. Jesus' baptism and temptation *(3–4)*

Jesus is baptized by his cousin John the Baptist, and tempted by Satan. Both events prepare him for his ministry on earth.

C. Sermon on the Mount *(5–7)*

This is one of Jesus' most famous sermons. The Beatitudes are here.

D. Jesus shows his power (8–9)

Jesus calms a storm, sends demons into a herd of pigs, heals a bleeding woman, and raises a girl from the dead.

E. Jesus trains and sends out disciples (10)

Jesus had called his disciples and trained them. Now he is sending them out to do his work.

F. Jesus is rejected (11–12)

The Temple leaders are jealous and scared of Jesus. They start giving him a hard time whenever they can.

G. Parables on growth (13)

Jesus teaches people by telling them stories. These stories are about a mustard seed, yeast, wheat and weeds, hidden treasure, a pearl and a fishing net.

H. Jesus shows his mission (14–17)

Jesus feeds over 5,000 people with five loaves and two fish, walks on the water, is transfigured on a mountain, and rescues a boy from demons. Peter declares that Jesus is the Messiah.

I. Jesus teaches about relationships *(18)*

Jesus tells the parable of the lost sheep and a man who went to jail because he would not forgive.

J. Jesus goes to Jerusalem *(19–23)*

Jerusalem was a special city in Israel. Jesus tells more parables, heals more people, answers questions and rides into town on a donkey as the crowd cheers.

K. Jesus teaches about the future *(21–25)*

Jesus tells about the final judgment and when he will come back to earth as the King.

L. Jesus' death and resurrection *(26:1–28:15)*

Jesus says good-bye to his disciples and gives his own life. God raises him from the dead, and the disciples get to see him again.

M. Jesus goes back to heaven *(28:16-20)*

Jesus commands his disciples (including us!) to go and make disciples.

FAQs

Q: Why was it important to prove that Jesus is the Messiah?

A: God made many promises in the Old Testament about the coming of the Messiah. In the New Testament, Jesus shows that God keeps his promises.

Q: What is the Sermon on the Mount?

A: The Sermon on the Mount is a very well-known part of Jesus' teaching. It includes the Beatitudes, the Lord's Prayer, and the Golden Rule *(see chapters 5–7)*.

LOOKOUT FOR . . .

As you read through Matthew, be on the lookout for . . .

Quotes from the Old Testament. Matthew quotes the Old Testament over 50 times and refers to it over 75 times!

Words of Jesus. Jesus' words are printed in red in some Bibles. Matthew tells us many sermons and stories that Jesus told.

Kingdom of Heaven. Matthew uses this phrase over 30 times. Matthew represents Jesus as King.

SPECIAL REPORT

Messiah. The Jewish people had been waiting for a Messiah. The Old Testament taught them over and over again that God would send someone to save them. The Jews thought that God would send a mighty warrior who would fight for them against their enemies. They were disappointed when God's Messiah turned out to be a  man who grew up near them and liked to teach them rather than fight for them.

Jesus was the Messiah they had waited for, and he will one day save us from all our enemies. But, first, he died for our sin to save us from ourselves.

STUDY QUESTIONS

• What did Jesus say about worry? *(Matthew 6:25-34)*

• Who is the greatest in the Kingdom of Heaven? *(Matthew 18:1-6)*

• One of the most famous passages in the Bible is *Matthew 28:16-20*. What do you think makes it so important?

MARK

WHY THIS BOOK?

Action is the key word for the book of Mark. Mark wrote his Gospel showing what Jesus did more than telling what he said. Mark was not a disciple of Jesus, but he probably was an eyewitness to what Jesus did. The Gospel of Mark may be the first of the New Testament books written. Some people think the other three Gospel writers quote from Mark.

The book of Mark is the shortest of the four Gospels. Yet it has more of Jesus' miracles than any of the others. Mark describes Jesus' life, death, burial, and resurrection. He gives these details of Jesus' life through pictures of Jesus as a servant.

Mark was writing to people who were not Jewish. They were Romans, Syrians, Greeks, and others who did not know about the coming of Messiah. The active service of Jesus helping people was meaningful for those people. When Jesus healed people from terrible diseases they could see he had come from the Father.

Jesus wanted to show God's love to the people so they would believe in him.

VITAL STATS/OUTLINE

A. Jesus is popular in Galilee *(1:1–3:12)*

John the Baptist prepares the way for Jesus and ushers him into the spotlight. Jesus begins to gather disciples and to heal people.

B. Jesus makes friends and enemies *(3:13–7:23)*

The leaders begin to dislike Jesus. They are afraid he will become more important than they are.

C. Jesus and his disciples *(7:24–9:50)*

187

Mark

Jesus continues to heal people and spends a lot of time teaching the disciples and preparing them for ministry.

D. The ministry in Judea *(10)*

Jesus travels to the south. He blesses children and heals more people.

E. Death and resurrection of Jesus *(11–16)*

Jesus returns to Jerusalem. He confronts the church leaders and has his last meal with the disciples. Then he is crucified. Three days later he rises from the dead.

FAQs

Q: Why did Mark write his book especially for non-Jewish people?

A: The Holy Spirit inspired people to write the word of God to meet the needs of different people. The Romans, Syrians, Greeks, and others who were not Jewish might not understand all the history and

promises God had made the Jews (see Matthew). But they could understand God's love shown through Jesus' actions toward people.

Q: How did Jesus treat people who were not God's chosen people, the Jews?

A: Jesus wanted everyone to experience God's love and forgiveness. He showed God's care for Jews and non-Jews alike by healing them, casting out demons, going to their towns and preaching, and sending his disciples to serve them.

LOOKOUT FOR . . .

As you read through Mark, be on the lookout for . . .

Explanations. Mark may have written this book for Christians who were not Jews. Because of this he explains Jewish traditions and customs.

Miracles. Mark records 18 of the 35 miracles that Jesus did.

"Immediately." Over 40 times Mark uses a word that means immediately or right away.

SPECIAL REPORT

The Resurrection. Mark's Gospel ends with the exciting story of the Resurrection. Jesus had died on the cross. He had been buried in a stone tomb with a very heavy rock rolled in front of the opening. Mark tells us that three ladies came to this tomb and found the stone rolled away and an angel nearby. The angel told them that Jesus was alive and was gone from the tomb.

The resurrection of Jesus is one of the most important facts in Christian history. Jesus died for our sins. But the fact that he came back to life means that he is greater than that sin and greater than death. It is because Jesus rose from the dead that we will live forever.

STUDY QUESTIONS

• How did the Ten Towns learn about Jesus' great power and care for people? *(Mark 5:1-20)*

• What did Jesus do for the many people who came to him with problems? *(Mark 6:53-56)*

• How does Jesus want us to pray? *(Mark 11:20-25)*

LUKE

WHY THIS BOOK?

Angels, shepherds, a stable, and a baby—what could these things mean but Christmas? And where does this best-known and most-favorite Bible story come from? The Gospel of Luke.

Luke gives many details about Jesus' birth and childhood that none of the other Gospels give. Luke, the man who wrote this book, was a Greek doctor. His Gospel shows how Jesus was the perfect man. It is clear that Jesus is God's Son because of the angel's announcement to Mary. But Luke also calls Jesus the Son of Man.

The books of Matthew, Mark, and Luke are called the Synoptic Gospels. That means "seeing the whole together at a glance." They all tell about Jesus from a slightly different angle.

Luke has some details that the other Gospels do not have. For example, Luke records several joyful songs of praise. One of these is Mary's song, praising God for what he was going to do for her and through her.

Several parables of Jesus are found only in Luke. They give a clear picture of God's love for the lost. The book of Luke also shows Jesus' tender care for women, who often were mistreated.

Luke

We learn a lot about Jesus from the book of Luke that we would not know without it.

VITAL STATS/OUTLINE

A. Jesus' birth, childhood, and roots *(1–3)*
Luke gives us information about the young Jesus that we cannot find anywhere else.

B. Jesus' ministry in Galilee *(4–9)*
Jesus teaches and heals around his own hometown.

C. Jesus' remaining ministry *(10–21)*
Jesus leaves his home for Jerusalem, the religious center for his people. The rest of his ministry happens there.

D. Jesus' sacrifice *(22–24)*
God the Son gives up his own life and God the Father raises him from the dead, just as Jesus said he would.

FAQs

Q: Why is it important that Jesus was a man?

A: He needed to be a perfect and sinless person in order to pay for the sins of all people. And as a man, he depended on the Holy Spirit to obey the Heavenly Father. He faced temptation just as we do. And he showed us what God is like and how God wants us to live.

Q: What did the angel tell Mary?

A: God sent the angel Gabriel to tell Mary that she was going to have a baby. But he would not be an ordinary baby born in an ordinary way. The Holy Spirit would form the Baby Jesus in Mary's womb, even though she was a virgin!

LOOKOUT FOR . . .

As you read through Luke, be on the lookout for . . .

Women. Luke mentions more women than any other Gospel.

The poor. Luke records many of Jesus' words about people who are poor.

Prayers. There are several prayers in the Gospel of Luke.

Songs. This book includes several songs, including Mary's and the angels'.

SPECIAL REPORT

The humanity of Christ. Jesus was God in the flesh. But he was also one hundred percent human. That is hard for our minds to understand, and that is why we call it a mystery. Luke's Gospel points out Christ's humanity over and over again.

Luke reveals Jesus' early years, when he grew up through childhood just as we do. Luke reveals Jesus' compassion for people who hurt as Jesus healed the people around him. Jesus wept when he saw Jerusalem because he knew they did not understand why he had come.

Jesus experienced life just as we do, with happiness and hurt. But he was also God, and he gave his human life so we could live forever.

STUDY QUESTIONS

• How did Simeon and Anna confirm Gabriel's message that Jesus was the Christ? (Luke 2:25-38)

• What are some ways Jesus showed his special care for women? (Luke 7:11-15; 7:36-50; 13:10-17)

• How did Jesus treat children? (Luke 18:15-17)

JOHN

WHY THIS BOOK?

Many people say Jesus never claimed to be God. They must not have read the book of John! This book was written by John, one of Jesus' closest disciples. John was with Jesus more than almost any other person. John was in Jesus' inner circle of friends and saw miracles that few others saw. He saw Jesus' glory when he was transfigured. John heard God the Father say, "This is my beloved Son, and I am fully pleased with him. Listen to him" *(Matthew 17:5).* John's message is clear: Jesus is the Son of God.

John lets his readers know that Jesus was the Word of God before time. Jesus is a separate Person from the Father, and he is God. Jesus is the Creator who made all that there is.

John reports the messages Jesus taught about himself. When Jesus made statements about himself using the words "I am," he was using words that God used in the Old Testament. Jesus said, "I am the bread of life . . . the light of the world . . . the gate

. . . the good shepherd." Jesus was telling people that he is the one to meet their deepest needs. He is the only one who can forgive sins and bring people into God's family.

John was at the cross when Jesus died. He was also one of the first to see the empty tomb after Jesus rose from the dead.

Anyone who wants to know who Jesus is can read an eyewitness report in the book of John.

VITAL STATS/OUTLINE

A. Christ in creation *(1:1-18)*

John has a beautiful and almost poetic beginning to his Gospel, tracing Jesus' roots all the way back to God himself. This is because John's purpose was to reveal Jesus as the Son of God.

B. Christ reveals who he is *(1:19–6:71)*

Jesus reveals himself by calling his disciples, doing miracles, walking on water, talking to a Samaritan woman, talking to Nicodemus, and clearing the merchants out of the Temple.

C. Christ and the Jews *(7–12)*

Jesus had some enemies among the leaders. Still he tried to explain to them that he was there to help them. He even raised Lazarus from the dead.

D. Christ and his disciples *(13–17)*

Jesus spends some time with just the disciples. He teaches them and eats his last meal with them.

E. Christ's death and resurrection *(18–21)*

Jesus is betrayed by Judas and arrested. He is crucified and buried. Then he rises from the dead and spends more time with his followers before he returns to heaven.

FAQs

Q: What does "transfigured" mean?

A: It means that Jesus suddenly looked different. Even though Jesus was God while he was on earth, people did not see his glory. But when Jesus was transfigured, his face shone and his clothes became dazzling white. He shone with the glory that belonged to him as God. John was one of the disciples who saw Jesus' glory.

Q: If Genesis says that God created the world, how can Jesus be the Creator?

A: Because Jesus is God.

Q: Why doesn't John tell everything that Jesus did?

A: None of the Gospel writers could tell everything that Jesus did. There would not be enough room. But they each give a picture of Jesus to show that he is God's Son, the Messiah/Savior.

LOOKOUT FOR . . .

As you read through John, be on the lookout for . . .

Christ as God. John has several clear statements that Jesus is God.

Key words. John uses these key words often: witness, believe (almost 100 times!), light, and love.

The Holy Spirit. John is the only gospel that teaches a lot about the Holy Spirit.

Word pictures. John uses word pictures that the other Gospels do not. For example, he calls Jesus the bread of life, the good shepherd, the light of the world, the way, the truth, and the life.

SPECIAL REPORT

Incarnation. Jesus was a human being like you. If he skinned his knees they would bleed. He had feelings. He had to learn to read and write. But through

a miracle that only God can understand, Jesus was also God. God came to live as a human being. That is called the Incarnation.

Jesus' life is the only time God has done this. He did it so that we could see that he wants to have a friendship with us. He wants that so much that he took the punishment for our sins on the cross. That was his part in the friendship.

Our part is to believe in him and to trust that he will do what he says. When we pray, we are showing we believe he is listening and that he will answer. That is why John wrote his Gospel . . . so that we would believe in Jesus, our God and Savior.

STUDY QUESTIONS

• What did another man named John say about Jesus? *(John 1:29-34)*

• How did Jesus' first miracle help his disciples believe in him? *(John 2:1-11)*

John

• What did Jesus pray for himself? *(John 17:1-5)*

• What did Jesus pray for his disciples and all future believers? *(John 17:6-26)*

ACTS

WHY THIS BOOK?

Whatever happened to the scared disciples who ran off into the night when Jesus was arrested? The book of Acts tells the story. It tells what happened after the risen Christ appeared to them and sent the Counselor (the Holy Spirit) to help them spread the Good News. It tells of the incredible events that followed after Jesus returned to heaven.

The book of Acts is the history of the early church. It tells how the church began and how it grew and spread from Jerusalem to the Roman world.

The scared disciples became brave spokesmen for Christ. They spoke to the religious leaders. They endured prison, beatings, and even death. But Christ's message of eternal life in God's family continued to spread.

A highly educated Jewish leader named Saul found out he was working against God. The Lord turned Saul's life upside down. Later he made three long trips to other countries to tell people about the Savior.

In addition to history, the

book of Acts tells what the Holy Spirit taught the Christians. The changed lives of the disciples and many others recorded in Acts give proof that Jesus Christ is who he said he is—the Son of God.

VITAL STATS/OUTLINE

A. Witnessing in Jerusalem *(1–7)*

Pentecost, the birth of the church. Peter preaches, the apostles heal some people, the church starts, Stephen becomes the first martyr.

B. Witnessing in Judea and Samaria *(8–12)*

Saul becomes a Christian, the gospel spreads, an angel rescues Peter from prison.

C. Witnessing in the Gentile world *(13–28)*

Paul's missionary journeys, his arrests, his arrival in Rome.

FAQs

Q: What happened to Jesus' brothers?

A: At first, Jesus' brothers did not believe in him. They taunted him and one time even thought he was out of his mind. But shortly

after his death and resurrection, they were in the upper room, along with their mother and other followers, waiting for the Holy Spirit. James, one of Jesus' brothers, became a leader in the church and also wrote the book of James.

Q: Why was the day of Pentecost such a big deal?

A: That is when the Holy Spirit came and filled the followers of Christ, the first Christians. There was noise like a loud rushing wind. Then there were what looked like tongues of fire that rested on each person. The people began to speak in languages they did not know. Those who listened could understand and many became Christians too. It was the first time God had come to live in his people in this way.

LOOKOUT FOR . . .

As you read through Acts, be on the lookout for . . .

The Holy Spirit. Christians get excited because the Holy Spirit comes to be with them just as Jesus said he would.

Decisions of the early church. The church leaders have to make many decisions about how they will lead and how they will do the work of the church.

Paul. Paul is a very important person in the second half of Acts.

SPECIAL REPORT

Pentecost. Pentecost was a Jewish festival that happened 50 days after the Passover. Jesus had been crucified on the Passover, then raised to life. He had appeared to his disciples, then went back into heaven. It was at this festival that the Holy Spirit—the counselor—first came to live inside God's people.

It is important to remember that the church in the time of Acts was in the middle of a big change. God's people were used to worshiping in the Temple, but Jesus had shown them that God was not just in the Temple. He was in them. They were used to offering sacrifices, but Jesus' death was the last sacrifice anyone would ever need. The coming of the Holy Spirit at Pentecost showed the early church that things would be different from then on.

STUDY QUESTIONS

• What were Jesus' final instructions to his disciples? (Acts 1:8)

• How did God use an earthquake to save a family? (Acts 16: 16-34)

ROMANS

WHY THIS BOOK?

Usually people write personal letters to people they know. But sometimes people write to strangers whom they want to get to know. They are called pen pals.

The apostle Paul was quite a pen pal. He had never met the people in the churches at Rome. But he had heard about them. He hoped to visit the Christians in Rome on a trip he planned to take to Spain. He wanted to introduce himself and explain Christian faith to the Roman believers. He wrote to them all about what it means to be a Christian.

The letter, or epistle, that Paul wrote is called the book of Romans. It clearly explains that everyone has sinned because everyone is a descendant of Adam. It also gives the Good News, or gospel, that Jesus Christ died and rose again to pay the penalty for our sin.

The book of Romans also tells about Israel, the church, spiritual gifts, faith, and the Christian life.

It was this book of the Bible that most helped Martin Luther. In the sixteenth century the church was teaching that people were saved by good works. Luther read in the book of Romans about God's grace. Grace is God's freely-given love. And faith is complete trust. Reading the book of Romans helped Luther trust Jesus as his Savior.

Other things people can learn from the book of Romans are that Christ frees us from sin, helps us to be like himself, and helps us live to please him.

VITAL STATS/OUTLINE

A. Why Paul is writing *(1:1-17)*

Paul explains that he is writing to the Romans because he wants to explain the gospel and what it means for their everyday lives.

B. We live in a lost world *(1:18–3:20)*
Paul writes to the Romans about the Jewish world as well as the Gentile world. He says that both worlds need the gospel.

C. We are justified by faith, not works *(3:21–5:21)*
Paul talks about many different truths here, but this is his main theme.

D. Live holy lives *(6–8)*
Even though we are accepted by God through faith, we still have to work to keep sin out of our lives.

E. The Jews *(9–11)*

God made some important promises to the Jews, and God is still going to keep those promises. The Jews have a special heritage. But salvation is for everyone, not just the Jews.

F. Christian conduct *(12:1–15:13)*

As Christians we are God's agents. We need to live lives that honor him.

G. Notes from Paul *(15:11–16:27)*

Remember, this is actually a letter. At the end Paul gives some newsy information and says some "hellos" to friends in Rome.

FAQs

Q: How did the people in Rome become Christians?

A: They may have heard the gospel from some Jews who had been in Jerusalem during Pentecost. When Peter and Jesus' other disciples received the Holy Spirit, they spoke freely about Christ. Many people heard the gospel and believed in Jesus. Then they took the Good News back to their homes.

Q: What does Adam's sin have to do with people now?

A: Adam is the father of all people. We have all inherited his sin nature. Even very good people cannot be good all the time and in every way.

Q: How can anyone be good enough to go to heaven?

A: No one but Jesus is good enough to go to heaven. That is why he died in our place

and why we need to trust him. Then he gives us his goodness and helps us do what is good and right.

LOOKOUT FOR . . .

As you read through Romans, be on the lookout for . . .

Faith. Paul talks a lot about faith because many Jews still think that if they keep enough rules they can please God that way instead of through faith.

Sin. Paul tells us the truth about sin: We all do it. We need God's forgiveness.

Abraham. Abraham is an important person in this book because he is an example to us all. Abraham did many good things to please God, but it was still his faith that pleased God most.

SPECIAL REPORT

Justification by faith. To be justified is to be found right or righteous. If someone gets angry for a good reason we say that his or her anger was justified. It was the right way to feel in that situation.

God is holy. That means he is not like anything or anyone else. It also means that he has no evil, no wrong, and no sin in him. Paul's question to the Romans was, "How can we, a sinful people, be justified (right or righteous) to a holy, sinless God?" Paul's answer was, "By our faith in Christ and in his death for our sins."

When we believe in God, in his son Jesus, and in Jesus' death and resurrection, we are giving God exactly what he wants—our faith. We believe him. We believe in him. That is what he asks of us. We are justified by our faith.

STUDY QUESTIONS

- How did Paul praise the Lord? *(Romans 11:33-36)*
- Since Jesus forgives sins, how should people behave? *(Romans 12:1-21)*

1 CORINTHIANS

WHY THIS BOOK?

A good father takes responsibility for his children. He teaches them right from wrong. He trains them to make good decisions. He warns them if he sees them in danger.

The apostle Paul was like a father to the Christians in Corinth. He lived in that city for many months during his second missionary trip. Paul told the people how Jesus died and rose again to save them from sin. Many of them believed and became Christians.

The book of 1 Corinthians is a letter Paul wrote to his spiritual children in Corinth. He wrote it from Ephesus during his third missionary journey. After Paul left Corinth, the people had problems putting their Christian faith into practice. They wrote to him asking for advice. Paul wrote 1 Corinthians to answer their questions and to give them more instructions.

Corinth was a large city by the sea. It had a temple to the goddess Aphrodite. It had a lot of idol worship, wealth, greed, and immorality. Before some of the people became Christians, they lived very sinful lives like their neighbors. After becoming Christians, they were not sure how to live.

So Paul wrote about topics that would help them, such as Christian unity, purity, marriage, spiritual gifts, worship, and the future resurrection. He also addressed it to "all Christians everywhere—whoever calls upon the name of Jesus Christ" (1 Corinthians 1:2b), so that others

would learn from it. Christians now and in the future can also learn from the advice and teaching in 1 Corinthians.

VITAL STATS/OUTLINE

A. Problems that Paul has heard about *(1–6)*

Paul confronts their fighting, immorality, lawsuits against each other, and basic lack of wisdom.

B. Problems the Corinthians had written to Paul about *(7–14)*

Paul responds to questions about marriage, food, worship, and spiritual gifts.

C. Explanation of the resurrection and eternal life *(15)*

Paul explains the resurrection of Christ and the resurrection of believers that will happen when Christ comes again.

D. Personal matters *(16)*

Paul gives instructions about donations. He also gives some news about people he and the Corinthians know.

FAQs

Q: What are spiritual gifts?

A: Spiritual gifts are special talents or abilities that God gives to Christians. Their purpose is to bring glory to God and to help other people. The Holy Spirit enables people to use their gifts. Some spiritual gifts are teaching, serving, faith, healing, miraculous powers, and prophecy.

Q: Why did Paul talk about Jesus' resurrection?

A: Some people doubted that Jesus really died. Others doubted that he came alive again. Paul made it clear that Jesus died, was buried, and rose again just as Scripture said he would. Paul also said

that Jesus appeared to Peter, the rest of the disciples, and then to more than 500 people at the same time. Jesus also appeared to his brother James, and finally he appeared to Saul (Paul). If Jesus had not risen from the dead, we would not be able to be forgiven of our sins.

LOOKOUT FOR . . .

As you read through 1 Corinthians, be on the lookout for . . .

Correction. Paul is writing to correct the Corinthians and to help them get rid of sin in their church.

Sins of the body. Paul points out many different ways we should be careful with our bodies, especially the food we eat and the way we deal with sex.

SPECIAL REPORT

Immorality. Morals are rules about the right way to live. If something is immoral, it is wrong or outside of the rules. The Corinthians were involved in immorality. They were involved in sin. Some of their sins were sexual sins. They were not keeping their sexual relationships between one husband and one wife. They were also immoral in the way they treated each other. They were not loving or kind. They were not getting along even to the point of suing each other instead of working out their differences.

Paul wrote to them about their immorality so they would change their ways. He also wrote to them about not accepting the immorality of other Christians in the church. He told them not to accept immorality in any way. Christians need to have high standards for their lives.

STUDY QUESTION

- What is so special about the gospel? *(1 Corinthians 1:18-25)*
- Why should a Christian show respect to every other Christian? *(1 Corinthians 12:4-26)*
- When is a Christian at his or her best? *(1 Corinthians 13)*
- How does Paul describe the resurrected bodies that Christians will have? *(1 Corinthians 15:42-57)*

2 CORINTHIANS

WHY THIS BOOK?

It is not fun to defend yourself against critics. The apostle Paul did not like to do it either. But he wrote 2 Corinthians to prove that God had called him to be an apostle just as he had called the original 12 disciples.

This letter was written within a year of 1 Corinthians. Instead of focusing on doctrine and theology, it tells of Paul's life and ministry. It is a very personal letter, telling how Paul feels about the problems he was facing. There were false teachers in Corinth who were trying to discredit Paul and his message about Christ.

Even though he did not want to defend himself, Paul reminded the Corinthians of how God had used him to bring them to Christ. He told of the ways he suffered for Christ in order to take them the gospel.

The Corinthian believers were still immature in many ways. Paul encouraged them to believe the truth instead of believing the false teachers. He did not want to find them living sinful lives the next time he visited them. He loved them and wanted them to live in fellowship with the Lord Jesus.

VITAL STATS/OUTLINE

A. Paul's ministry *(1-7)*

Paul thanks God for his comfort during hardships and tells the Corinthians about some of his decisions in ministry.

B. Donations *(8-9)*

The benefits of generous giving and a reminder of the commitments the Corinthians have made.

C. Paul's defense against false apostles *(10-12)*

Paul states his authority and discredits the false teachers who have lied about him.

D. Closing matters *(13)*

Paul gives some final advice.

FAQs

Q: What kinds of things did Paul suffer?

A: Paul suffered beatings, imprisonment, riots, hard work, sleepless nights, and hunger. He even had to be lowered over a city wall in a large basket to escape from thugs.

Q: What were the false teachers teaching?

A: The false teachers were not telling the truth about Jesus.

They were teaching about a different "Jesus" and "Holy Spirit." They were saying there was a different way of salvation. They were very good speakers, but what they were saying was untrue.

Q: What were the false teachers saying about Paul?

A: The false teachers were saying that Paul was not a good speaker. They said he wrote "bold" letters but was very "timid" in person. They said he was weak, and they tried to lure the Christians away from listening to him.

LOOKOUT FOR . . .

As you read through 2 Corinthians, be on the lookout for . . .

Personal news. This is a very personal letter of Paul's. If you read closely you can learn a lot about him from the things he shares about himself.

Difficult times. Paul shares many of his own difficulties and how God has helped him through them.

2 Corinthians

SPECIAL REPORT

Thorn in the flesh. We do not know what Paul was referring to in chapter 12 by his "thorn in the flesh." We do know that it was something wrong with him. He prayed for God to take it away, but God did not. Because of some of the things Paul says in other places, it may have been a problem with his eyes. It affected the way he looked as well as causing him inconvenience and pain.

But Paul did not let his "thorn in the flesh" hold him back. He still loved people and served them. People sometimes say, "That's my thorn in the flesh." It is fine for them to say that as long as they are not using it as an excuse to give up. Paul's thorn never made him give up.

STUDY QUESTIONS

     • What warnings did Paul give the Corinthian church?
(2 Corinthians 13:1-10)

     • What was neat about Paul's farewell to the Corinthians?
(2 Corinthians 13:11-14)

GALATIANS

WHY THIS BOOK?

Some people like rules. They think they keep all the rules so well that they are good, really good. But people who think they can keep all the rules really just fool themselves. No one can keep all of life's rules.

The apostle Paul wrote the book of Galatians to help people understand that it is not rule keeping that makes a person a Christian.

Paul had visited Galatia (now in the land of Turkey). He preached the gospel to Gentiles, people who are not Jews. They put their faith in Jesus and became Christians.

But some other Christians said that their faith in Jesus was not enough. They said that all Christians had to keep the law of Moses in order to be saved. But Paul's letter explained that trying to keep the law of Moses did not save anybody, not even the Jews, because no one can keep the law. Only faith in Jesus can save a person. So Paul told the Galatians that they did not need to keep the law of Moses. They did not need to be just like Jews.

What was true for the Galatians is true for us too: Jesus is the only person who could keep the whole Law. By trusting in Jesus, we become good in God's eyes. It is as if we never sinned! That was good news for the Galatians, and it is good news for us, too.

VITAL STATS/OUTLINE

A. Two problems (1–2)
Paul writes to correct two wrong ideas. One is that people must

obey the Jewish customs and laws to be children of God. The second is that Paul is not really an apostle.

B. We are justified by faith (3–4)

Paul spends a lot of time explaining to the Galatians that we become God's children through faith in Jesus, no matter how good we are or how many laws we follow.

C. We are free in Christ (5–6)

Because we are justified by faith and not our good deeds, we are free to be loved by God no matter what we have done.

FAQs

Q: What were the rules the Jews had to keep?

A: The Jews had many ceremonial laws about worship, food, work, and cleanliness. Paul said God used the law like a schoolteacher to show people they cannot be good enough without Jesus.

Q: Did Jesus get rid of the law?

A: Jesus said he did not come to destroy the law but to fulfill it. He is the only one who is perfect and could do everything to please God the Father.

Q: What would happen if the Galatians tried to keep the law?

A: Nothing. It would not help them, because no one can be saved by keeping the law.

LOOKOUT FOR . . .

As you read through Galatians, be on the lookout for . . .

The law. Jews have a lot of laws and customs. Paul says a lot about the Christian's responsibility to those laws and customs.

Freedom. Paul intently wants Christians to have freedom and joy in Christ. He mentions this a lot.

Faith. Paul explains faith in many of his writings, but he explains it a lot in Galatians.

SPECIAL REPORT

Judaizers. Way back in the Old Testament God promised a man named Abraham that he would become the father of a great nation. That nation was the Jewish nation. They had many laws and customs and a special relationship with God. God was going to bring the Messiah, Jesus, from that group of people.

But when Jesus died on the cross, he died for everyone's sin, not just the Jews'. After Jesus went back to heaven, some of the apostles preached the Good News of salvation not only to the Jews, but also to the Gentiles. This made some people very upset. They felt that a person must become a Jew or at least obey

Galatians

Jewish customs to really be a child of God. These people were called Judaizers and they were a lot of the reason Paul wrote Galatians.

STUDY QUESTIONS

• How should a person use the freedom Christ gives? *(Galatians 5:13-21)*

• How should a Christian behave? *(Galatians 5:22-26)*

EPHESIANS

WHY THIS BOOK?

Who would expect to hear good news from someone in jail? Most people in jail are sad, angry, or bitter. The apostle Paul was in jail in Rome for teaching and preaching about Jesus, but his letters were filled with good news!

The letter to the Ephesians was a message of encouragement for the Christians in Ephesus. Paul wrote this letter to teach and encourage the church at Ephesus as well as other churches nearby.

Ephesians is filled with praise to God for his gift of salvation. It tells about Jesus Christ as the head of all Christians everywhere. All people who believe in Jesus are part of his body, the church. Another way to say it is that Christians are in a new family—God's family.

Paul told many of the benefits of being part of God's family. He also instructed his readers how to live in ways that please God. Ephesians has important information about the way people should behave in families.

Paul knew that the Devil is real

and that Christians are in a spiritual battle against him. But Paul encouraged believers to put on the spiritual armor of God in order to stand against the enemy. Today people still read Ephesians to be encouraged and to learn how to honor God.

VITAL STATS/OUTLINE

A. Greetings *(1:1-2)*
Paul usually says who he is and who he is writing to at the beginning of his letters.

B. Beliefs of the church *(1:3–3:21)*
Salvation comes from Jesus, wisdom comes from God, we are alive in Christ, we are one in Christ, we are Christ's body, God is going to change the world through us.

C. Actions of the church *(4–6)*
Humility, gentleness, unity, truthfulness, honor, purity, godly homes, strong families, good workers, strong spiritual people prepared for spiritual warfare.

FAQs

Q: What's so great about being in God's family?
A: A person who is in God's family is alive in Christ, has God's

mercy and salvation, has Christ's power to obey God and to love others, and can call God "Father."

Q: What is the armor a Christian should wear?

A: The armor Paul told Christians to put on is a belt of truth, body armor of righteousness, shoes of peace, a shield of faith, and a helmet of salvation. He said to use the Bible as a sword against Satan and to pray all the time.

LOOKOUT FOR . . .

As you read through Ephesians, be on the lookout for . . .

God's plan for us. Ephesians tells us a lot about how God wants to use us.

Personal qualities. Ephesians lists many qualities that we should have in our lives.

The church. Paul tells the Ephesians all about the church and what God has planned for it.

SPECIAL REPORT

Spiritual warfare. A spiritual war is a war that is against Satan and evil, not against another country or person. Ephesians 6:10-18 is one of the most famous passages on spiritual warfare. It tells us to be prepared. It uses the different pieces of armor to describe the tools we need to fight evil. Truth is described as a belt. Peace from the gospel is described as shoes. Faith is described as a shield. Salvation is described as a helmet. The Bible is described as a sword. Prayer does not have a word picture, but it is also mentioned as an important way to fight evil around you and around the world.

STUDY QUESTIONS

• How do good deeds help a person get saved? *(Ephesians 2:8-10)*

• What are some of the reasons Christians should do good deeds? *(Ephesians 4:20-24)*

• What special advice does this letter have for children and parents? *(Ephesians 6:1-4)*

PHILIPPIANS

WHY THIS BOOK?

Some people think only good times and new things bring happiness. When bad things happen, they say things like, "It's been a bad day. I hope tomorrow is better." They might get angry or they may complain. They may even hurt someone else to take out their anger.

But people who depend on Jesus for joy can have his joy no matter what happens. Joy sometimes is bubbly and full of laughter. But sometimes it is just a quiet confidence that God is with us no matter what happens.

Paul wrote the letter of Philippians to the church in Philippi. He wrote about his own joy even while in jail in Rome. He could be joyful even when people were against him. He knew that God had allowed him to be in jail so the gospel could be preached there.

Paul wrote that to follow Christ's example and serve others brings real joy. Paul reminded the church in Philippi that Jesus is the only true source of joy. Compared to Jesus, everything else is trash.

Paul's letter to the Christians in Philippi was also a thank you note. They had sent him a gift of money. Paul was thankful for the

Christians' desire to be part of his ministry. It was their attitude of love that gave him joy.

Have you ever been miserable? The book of Philippians can give you a reason to be joyful.

VITAL STATS/OUTLINE

A. Greetings and thanksgiving *(1:1-20)*

Paul is very close to the people in the Philippian church. He thanks God for them.

B. Suffering for Christ *(1:21-30)*

Paul has suffered a lot, including being in jail for his faith. Still he believes in Christ's mercy and God's goodness.

C. Living the Christian life (2)

Humility, thankfulness, and the examples of Timothy and Epaphroditus

D. Knowing Christ (3)

Some people call this Paul's statement of faith. He says the most important thing in life is knowing Christ and spending every day getting to know Jesus better.

E. Paul's good-bye (4)

Paul loves these people and takes his time telling them thanks. He also tells them to be strong and happy.

FAQs

Q: Why were some people against Paul?

A: Some preachers were jealous of Paul. They thought they could cause him trouble by preaching, too. They also wanted to make a name for themselves. Paul was glad the message of Jesus was told—even if some people's motives were wrong.

Q: How did Paul preach the gospel if he was in jail?

A: Paul spoke to the Roman soldiers who were guarding him. People who probably would never have gone to hear him preach heard him every day. Also, other Christians became brave when they saw Paul's courage to speak up for the Lord.

LOOKOUT FOR . . .

As you read through Philippians, be on the lookout for . . .

Blessing of Christ. Paul talks a lot about the good things we have because of Jesus' life and death.

Love. See all the ways in which Paul expresses his love and encouragement to the Philippians.

SPECIAL REPORT

Philippi. Philippi was a city in ancient Macedonia. Macedonia belonged both to the Romans and the Greeks. Its greatest leader was King Philip, who was the father of Alexander the Great. Macedonia

was the first part of Europe to hear the gospel. Paul was the one to bring it there. He meant a lot to the Christians of Macedonia and its cities.

Philippi was an important city. It was probably the hometown of Luke, the doctor who wrote the Gospel of Luke. Paul may have picked Philippi for his missionary journey because so many roads went through it. If all of Macedonia was going to hear the gospel, Philippi was a great place to start.

STUDY QUESTIONS

• What are Christians supposed to think about and do? (Philippians 4:8-9)

• How should Christians handle money? (Philippians 4:11-13)

COLOSSIANS

WHY THIS BOOK?

For some people the gospel of Jesus Christ is just too simple. They want to make it complicated. They think there should be "secret knowledge" and special ceremonies that a person must do to be saved.

The apostle Paul wrote the letter to the Colossians to get rid of that mixed up idea. For example, false teachers were telling the Colossians that they had to eat and drink certain things and worship in special ways in order to be Christians. But Paul said that having faith in Jesus Christ is what makes a person a Christian.

The false teachers also taught that people needed to worship angels in order to get to God. But Jesus is the only one we need to reach the Father. Today, many people are interested in angels again. Angels are God's messengers, but we are not to worship them.

Another wrong idea the false teachers were teaching is that the body is evil. They said it does not matter what Christians do with

their bodies. But Paul explained that Jesus created people's bodies, and Christians should use their bodies in ways that are pure and holy.

Singing to God, living at peace with others, and doing everything to glorify Jesus Christ are some of the instructions Paul gave to the Colossian Christians. These are also important for believers today.

VITAL STATS/OUTLINE

A. Greetings and thanks *(1:1-14)*

Paul usually tells who he is at the beginning of the letter. Here he also gives some news, just like you would if you were writing to a friend.

B. Christ is above everything else *(1:15-29)*

The Colossians need to understand that Christ is God, only Christ died for our sins, and only Christ is worthy of our worship.

C. What to believe *(2)*

Several false teachings have come up. Some people worship angels. Some people put too many harsh rules on themselves. Some people have too much pride. Paul talks about each of these problems.

D. How to live in Christ *(3:1–4:6)*

This is the Good News. Paul points out that since Christ is above all and has forgiven our sins, we have wonderful lives to live.

We also have a responsibility to make wise choices and to love one another.

E. Final good-byes *(4:7-18)*

Paul finishes his letter much like you would. He gives some news and some instructions, like when someone writes to you and says, "My friend says hi."

FAQs

Q: Why did Paul remind the Christians that Jesus is God?

A: False teachers were saying that the body is evil so God would not come in bodily form. Paul made it clear that Jesus is God and man at the same time.

Q: Why did the false teachers want people to have special ceremonies and rules?

A: The false teachers wanted their own religion because it made them feel important.

LOOKOUT FOR . . .

As you read through Colossians, be on the lookout for . . .

Titles and traits of Christ. Paul uses a lot of different titles for Jesus because Jesus does and is so many things in our lives.

Doctrine, beliefs. Paul is writing to correct some false teachings. Because of this you will find a lot of writing about different beliefs.

Instructions to family members. Paul tells us some ways to be good family members.

SPECIAL REPORT

Heresy. A heresy is a strong opinion that a person holds even though it is not true. Many of Paul's letters were written because some heresy had slipped into a church, and he wanted to send a warning so the church would know how to tell the truth from error.

The church at Colosse was facing three particular heresies. One was the worship of angels. People were worshiping angels instead of only God. (This church continued to struggle with this for a long time even though Paul told them to be careful.) They also were struggling with legalism. They were trusting special rules to make them righteous and acceptable to God. They also were becoming proud and arrogant.

They were not trusting in Christ's goodness.

STUDY QUESTIONS

• What instructions did Paul give for Christian living? *(Colossians 3:1-17)*

• How are Christian families supposed to live? *(Colossians 3:18-21)*

1 THESSALONIANS

WHY THIS BOOK?

The church at Thessalonica was a young church. It began as a result of Paul's preaching during his second missionary trip. About two or three years later, he wrote the letter now called 1 Thessalonians.

Paul assured the believers that he prayed for them often. He encouraged them to continue in their faith in the Lord. He reminded them of how he had lived and worked with them and how much he loved them. Paul said he was like a mother to the believers, and he missed them.

The city of Thessalonica was an important, busy place. Idol worship was common there, and Christians were persecuted. Paul wanted to know if the believers remained faithful to Christ. He sent Timothy to encourage the Christians. In return, Paul was encouraged to learn they were still following the Lord.

But one thing troubled the Christians. They did not understand why it was taking Jesus so long to return. Paul told them that no one but the Father knows when Jesus will come back. Paul's advice was that they should continue living holy lives to please God.

The Thessalonians were also concerned about the people they loved who had already died. Would those who had died miss Jesus' return? Paul assured the Christians that believers who died would be the first to rise and return with Jesus. The job of those who are still alive is to live pure, productive, peaceful lives.

VITAL STATS/OUTLINE

A. The conversion of the Thessalonians *(1)*
When the Thessalonians came to believe in Christ they wholeheartedly followed him.

B. The beginning of the church in Thessalonica *(2)*
Paul shares his memories of when he and Silas helped start the

church.

C. Paul's concern and instruction for the church *(3:1–4:12)*

Paul is very concerned because of the suffering the church has gone through.

D. Jesus' return *(4:13–5:11)*

Paul explains that Christians who have died will be raised to life when Jesus comes back.

E. Paul's final instructions *(5:12-28)*

Paul reminds them to love each other and to live for Christ.

FAQs

Q: Why didn't Paul go himself to see the Christians in Thessalonica?

A: Paul said that Satan stopped him from going back to Thessalonica *(2:18)*. Paul does not explain what happened or how Satan kept him from returning.

Q: Who was Timothy?

A: Timothy was a fellow worker with Paul. He often traveled with Paul during his missionary trips. Timothy sometimes carried letters from Paul to other believers.

LOOKOUT FOR . . .

As you read through 1 Thessalonians, be on the lookout for . . .

1 Thessalonians

Jesus' return. Paul writes a lot about this. Notice that chapters 1–4 all close with comments about the return of Christ.

Paul's instructions. Paul reminds the people several times how they are to treat each other and live for Christ.

SPECIAL REPORT

The Second Coming. When Jesus came to earth to die for our sins he was born into the world as a baby. That is called the Incarnation. The next time Jesus comes to earth he will come as a king to take us home to heaven. That is called the Second Coming.

The Thessalonians had many questions about the Second Coming. That's a big reason why Paul wrote this book in the first place, as well as 2 Thessalonians. We are still looking forward to the Second Coming. The Bible tells us in many places, including the Thessalonian letters, to live holy lives so we can be ready to meet Christ face-to-face when he comes.

STUDY QUESTION

• What encouragement did Paul give the Thessalonians about the second coming of Jesus? *(1 Thessalonians 4:13-18)*

2 THESSALONIANS

WHY THIS BOOK?

Waiting can be hard. Sometimes people become impatient when they think someone is late. Some of the Christians in Thessalonica were confused about the second coming of Jesus. They misunderstood Paul's first letter to them. They thought Paul told them Jesus would come back any minute. They decided to stop everything else they were doing and just wait.

Paul wrote a second letter to the Thessalonians to help them understand what he meant. He wanted them to be active in their waiting. He was glad they believed in Jesus, but he did not want them just to sit and do nothing. Some people were not even working to provide for their families or themselves. Instead of being busy at work, they puttered around and gossiped.

The advice Paul gave was strong. He said, "Whoever does not work should not eat." Paul said the believers should warn other believers who were refusing to work.

Paul wanted the Christians to watch and work while waiting for Christ's return. The book of 2 Thessalonians gives believers today good advice about how to live while waiting for Jesus to come again—work hard!

VITAL STATS/OUTLINE

A. Greetings and appreciation (1)

The Thessalonians had stood strong during persecution and Paul told them so.

B. The Second Coming (2)

Paul tells the Thessalonians not to worry that the end has begun and gives them the signs of Jesus' coming.

C. Instructions and helpful words (3)

Paul encourages the church to stay busy doing good.

FAQs

Q: Why did the Thessalonians think Jesus was coming any minute?

A: A lot of Christians were in big trouble with the government. Roman officials did not like Christians and were allowed to hurt them, harass them, and even kill them—just for being Christians. So the

2 Thessalonians

Thessalonian Christians thought that Jesus would be returning any minute, to rescue them.

Q: What should we do while waiting for Jesus to return?

A: We should do everything God has asked of us. We should work at our jobs, obey God, serve God, take care of our families, tell others about Jesus, help the needy, pray faithfully, love others, build up the church, and do good.

LOOKOUT FOR . . .

As you read through 2 Thessalonians, be on the lookout for . . .

Signs of the Second Coming. Particularly in chapter two, Paul explains these signs so we can be prepared.

Persecution. Some people were harassing Christians just because they were Christians. Paul wrote encouraging words to these Christians.

SPECIAL REPORT

The Antichrist. John mentions the antichrist in 1 and 2 John. While this is the only time the actual word is used, Paul is talking about the same person in 2 Thessalonians 2:8 when he talks about the "man of lawlessness." In fact, ever since Old Testament days God's people have known about a person or power at the end of time who will attack them. That attack will be crushed by Jesus, the Messiah.

Paul described the antichrist in 2 Thessalonians because he wanted the Christians in Thessalonica to understand that the antichrist had not come yet, so Christ's coming was not about to happen in the next days or weeks. He gave them a sign to look for so they could continue working until Christ came.

STUDY QUESTION

• What did Paul say would happen before Jesus Christ returns? (2 Thessalonians 2:1-12)

1 TIMOTHY

WHY THIS BOOK?

Being young can be lots of fun. Young people have energy and strength that leave older people in awe. But sometimes young people can make mistakes just because they do not know any better.

When the apostle Paul was older he wrote to Timothy to give him advice. Timothy was a young pastor. Paul wanted Timothy to do a good job leading the church at Ephesus. Paul wrote to him about what was important. His letter is called 1 Timothy. It has good advice for church leaders and other Christians even today. Paul said that doctrine, or what people believe, is very important. He did not want Christians to get mixed up and believe lies about Jesus or about being a Christian. He told Timothy to be sure to pray for rulers so the Christians could live peaceful lives.

The life of the church is also very important. Paul gave Timothy advice about how believers should worship God. He also gave direction on choosing church leaders. Churches are made up of all ages of people and people in different circumstances. Paul advised Timothy how to treat people kindly yet firmly. The book of 1 Timothy is a good guidebook for any Christian learning to serve the Lord and his people.

VITAL STATS/OUTLINE

A. Greetings and instruction (1)
Paul asks Timothy to stay at Ephesus and deal with the teachers who are not doing right.

B. Instructions for worship (2)
A call to pray and to prepare for worship.

C. Instructions for church leaders (3)

Elders and deacons must live holy and respectable lives.

D. How to handle false teachers (4)

Timothy should take a stand against false teachers by teaching the truth.

E. Instructions on how to treat each other (5:1–6:2)

Treat elders with respect and take care of widows.

F. Final instructions: riches and a godly life (6:3-21)

People should concentrate more on loving God than on getting money.

FAQs

Q: Why did Paul think he should give Timothy advice?

A: Paul and Timothy were very close friends. Paul thought of Timothy as a son. Timothy helped Paul in his ministry. Paul knew that being a pastor is a big responsibility, and he wanted to encourage Timothy.

Q: Why is it important to pray for government leaders?

A: If government leaders do good, everyone benefits. They make good laws and make it easier for everyone to have a peaceful life.

LOOKOUT FOR . . .

As you read through 1 Timothy, be on the lookout for . . .

Worship guidelines. Paul tells Timothy how to lead the church in worship.

Advice and instructions. Paul is a friend and teacher to Timothy, so he gives him a lot of great advice.

Reasons. Paul does not just tell Timothy what to do. He also tells him why he needs to do it that way.

SPECIAL REPORT

Elders and deacons. Elders and deacons both served as church leaders in Timothy's day as well as in many churches today.

Elders were also called "bishops" or "overseers." They were to have clean reputations and live blameless lives. Their role in the church was to keep an eye on the spiritual growth of the congregation and the teaching of the Word. Today some churches have a "board" of several elders. Some churches just have their pastor as an elder.

Deacons were servant leaders. The first deacons took care of feeding the church so that the apostles had more time to teach. Today the deacons sometimes help make decisions in the church and have more responsibilities than church members who are not deacons.

Paul's words to Timothy are still the qualities of good church leaders.

STUDY QUESTIONS

• What kind of people should be leaders in the church? (*1 Timothy 3:1-13*)

• How did Paul say Timothy should treat the various people in the church? (*1 Timothy 5:1-21*)

2 TIMOTHY

WHY THIS BOOK?

Telephones are great. People can talk to each other clear around the world. With cellular phones, people can talk from cars, airplanes, or the middle of the jungle! Hearing the voice of someone you love is a special gift.

But letters are special, too. A letter is something you can hold in your hand. You can read it over and over again—even after the sender is no longer alive.

The apostle Paul was in prison waiting to be executed for his faith in Christ. Paul wrote his last letter to Timothy. It is in the Bible as 2 Timothy. Timothy was the young pastor whom Paul taught. Paul loved Timothy like a son. He wrote to Timothy to remind him how to be a good pastor. He encouraged him to remain true to Paul's teachings about Christ. Paul told Timothy to pass on to other faithful people the Good News about Jesus. Then they could teach others. That is how we received the message of Christ down through the ages.

One of the main things Paul emphasized for Timothy to teach is that Jesus is completely God and completely man at the same time.

2 Timothy

Paul warned that many people will not want to hear the truth. But Timothy was to continue teaching God's truth anyway.

Paul also shows his great love for Scripture. He told Timothy that the Bible is inspired by God. It is a Christian's guidebook for living the Christian life. Paul asked Timothy to visit him in prison and to bring his "papers" to him. The papers were probably some copies of Old Testament books. It is through reading and knowing God's Word that Paul strengthened his faith in Christ. The Holy Spirit kept the Bible safe for people to read today, too.

VITAL STATS/OUTLINE

A. Timothy, be faithful (1)

Paul tells Timothy to live his life by the good teaching he has received. We need to do the same thing.

B. Be a good soldier (2)

Work hard for Christ, being faithful in the hard parts of life and staying away from silly arguments.

C. The last days (3:1-9)

Be ready for difficult times. Some things will get

worse and worse as the world gets older.

D. Paul's good-bye and final words *(3:10–4:22)*

Paul tells Timothy to be strong for God. He also tells Timothy some newsy things such as whom to say hello to and to please visit soon.

FAQs

Q: What proof did Paul give that Jesus is both God and man?

A: Paul reminded Timothy that Jesus rose from the dead and that he was a descendant of King David.

Q: Why didn't Paul have his papers with him in prison?

A: Paul probably was arrested and taken to prison in a hurry and could not take his things with him.

LOOKOUT FOR . . .

As you read through 2 Timothy, be on the lookout for . . .

Advice. Paul writes this letter to give Timothy important advice. It is good advice for us, too.

Difficult times. Paul has been through some rough times: jail, beatings, huge disappointments, now prison. He tries to prepare Timothy for those kinds of trouble.

People. Paul mentions 27 people in this letter. This is more than any other letter of Paul's.

2 Timothy

SPECIAL REPORT

Paul's imprisonment. Paul wrote this letter when he was in prison, waiting to be executed. He had not done anything wrong. He was in prison for telling others about Jesus. He had been under arrest once before, but he had been released. This time he had no reason to believe that would happen.

Paul did not have many visitors. People were afraid to see him. So Paul was alone, in prison, probably in chains, waiting to die. But he did not just get depressed and give up. He wrote to Timothy so that Timothy could keep doing the work that Paul had started.

That is what makes this letter special. We know that Paul told Timothy the things that were most important to him because it may have been one of his last chances to do that. Paul wrote so that Timothy could be strong. We can read this letter and be strong, too.

STUDY QUESTIONS

• What did Paul say people will be like in the last days? *(2 Timothy 3:1-5)*

• How did Paul describe Scripture? *(2 Timothy 3:16)*

• How did Paul face his coming death? *(2 Timothy 4:7-8)*

TITUS

WHY THIS BOOK?

A good leader knows his limits. He knows he cannot do everything alone. He needs to rely on others.

Paul was facing execution by the Roman government because of his faith in Jesus. Titus was a Greek believer who had traveled with Paul during some of his missionary journeys. When Paul needed a strong leader for the churches on the island of Crete, he sent Titus. He instructed Titus to help the believers develop a strong church. The letter that Paul wrote to Titus is called the book of Titus. It is the third letter to pastors (the other two are 1 Timothy and 2 Timothy).

Titus also needed help serving the church. Paul gave him advice about what kind of people should be leaders. He made it clear that church leaders have to be people who study God's Word. They also must follow Jesus Christ. Titus would have to be on guard against false teachers.

Paul gave Titus other instructions, too. He told Titus how the believers should live. Once a person is a follower of Christ, he or she should want to do what is right in order to please God.

VITAL STATS/OUTLINE

A. Qualifications for church leaders *(1:1-9)*

Church leaders should be loving people who consider God in everything they do.

B. Warnings against false teachers *(1:10-16)*

Church leaders should warn their people about false teaching.

C. Right living in the church *(2)*

Because of God's grace we need to teach each other and do what is right.

D. Right living in society *(3)*

When we obey the law of the land, we help others see God's life in us.

FAQs

Q: Why did the churches on Crete need strong leaders?

A: The people of Crete were known for being lazy and undisciplined. The Christians there needed extra help learning to be good workers. This would make them good examples of God's grace and of how God changes people.

Q: Are there any other letters to church leaders like Titus?

A: 1 and 2 Timothy are also letters to a church leader.

LOOKOUT FOR . . .

As you read through Titus, be on the lookout for . . .

The qualities of a Christian leader. This is why Paul wrote to Titus.

God's grace and salvation. Paul gives this as our reason for living godly lives.

SPECIAL REPORT

Crete. Crete is an island just below the country of Greece. It was a large and prosperous island with almost one hundred cities when Paul was alive. Paul and his friends had started churches in many of those cities. But when Paul left, someone needed to be there to help those people grow.

Paul tells Titus that the Cretans (people who lived in Crete) were described as liars, lazy, and cruel. Titus had a lot of work to do to help the people of Crete to understand how to follow God and obey him, rather than live the way most Cretans did. But Titus had worked with difficult people before, and that may be the reason Paul sent him to this troubled place.

STUDY QUESTIONS

- What should church leaders be like? (*Titus 1:6-9*)
- What were the false teachers like? (*Titus 1:10-16*)
- How should Christians live? (*Titus 2:1-15*)

PHILEMON

WHY THIS BOOK?

Usually it is not polite to read someone else's mail. But the Holy Spirit had a special plan for a certain letter Paul wrote. It is the letter Philemon sent to Paul's friend in Colosse. It is also part of the New Testament.

Philemon was probably a rich Christian because the church met in his home and he also had slaves. Paul wrote this letter to ask Philemon to forgive his runaway slave Onesimus. Onesimus had fled to Rome, then met Paul and become a Christian.

Paul told Philemon that he prayed for him and thanked God for Philemon's love for believers. Then Paul told Philemon that his slave Onesimus had become a believer. Paul asked Philemon to accept Onesimus back as a brother. Paul could have ordered Philemon to do the right thing, because Paul was an apostle. But instead, Paul appealed to Philemon's love for him.

VITAL STATS/OUTLINE

A. Paul's greeting *(1:1-3)*

Usually in Paul's letters he starts out by saying who he is and who he is writing to.

B. Paul speaks well of Philemon *(1:4-7)*

Philemon has been a loving and kind person.

C. Paul asks a favor *(1:8-21)*

Philemon should forgive Onesimus because of God's command to love and forgive others.

D. Paul's good-bye *(1:22-24)*

Paul mentions some friends.

FAQs

Q: Why did the church meet in Philemon's house?

A: He was a kind and generous man who wanted to help the church. They did not have a church building, so they met in Philemon's house. That's the way most early churches did it.

Philemon

Q: Why did Philemon have a slave?

A: Slavery was common at that time. Paul asked Philemon to receive Onesimus back as a brother.

LOOKOUT FOR . . .

As you read through Philemon, be on the lookout for . . .

Reasons. The reasons Paul gives Philemon for showing kindness to Onesimus.

A favor. Paul is asking a favor as well as reminding Philemon of the favor Paul did for him.

SPECIAL REPORT

Slaves. Slaves were common in the Roman world of Paul's time. Some people sold themselves into slavery to pay off debts. Some of these people were treated more like servants than slaves. Many young girls were sold as slaves to be maids or handmaidens and to take care of a household or children.

There were laws governing the treatment

of slaves, but some slaves still got bad treatment because they were considered property. Paul did not write a letter trying to abolish slavery. But what he did was point out that God made us all and when God commands us to love it means we are to love everyone, no matter who they are or what society thinks of them.

STUDY QUESTION

• How did Paul think Philemon would respond? *(Philemon 1:21)*

HEBREWS

WHY THIS BOOK?

The book of Hebrews was written to Jewish Christians who were wondering if it might be better to go back to their old Jewish faith. These were Christians during the first century. They may have been wondering why Jesus had not returned yet to set up his kingdom. The writer of Hebrews makes it clear that everything about Jesus Christ is better than any other leader or religion. Jesus is superior to the prophets, angels, Moses, the Jewish priests, and the whole Old Testament way of serving God. Jesus is better because he is God. Jesus is better because he fulfills all the prophecies and all the laws. The writer of Hebrews said that the people should have been strong, mature Christians by the time he wrote the letter. But they were still like babies needing milk. He encouraged them to practice doing good so that they would be strong and able to resist temptation.

The book of Hebrews is probably best known for chapter 11. Many believers of the past are listed in this "Hall of Faith." For two thousand years it has encouraged Christians to trust in God.

Christians today can read the book of Hebrews and be reminded to stay true to Christ because he is the best.

VITAL STATS/OUTLINE

A. Christ is above everything else (1:1–4:13)

Christ is greater than the angels and greater than Moses.

B. The priesthood of Jesus Christ (4:14–10:18)

Jesus is the greatest high priest who ever lived in the past and who ever will live.

C. Christians must endure (10:19–12:29)

Examples of people who believe God (had faith). Encouragement to hold on to our faith no matter what.

D. Good-byes and personal notes (13:1-25)

Encouragement to live obedient lives.

FAQs

Q: Why would the Jewish Christians want to give up their faith in Jesus?

A: Everybody thinks fondly of the past sometimes. That is what these Jewish Christians were doing. They remembered the old ways and wondered if they were OK after all. And God had given the Hebrew people his revelation in the Old Testament; it had been the best up to that point. But they were forgetting that Jesus was indeed better.

Q: How does Hebrews say that Jesus is best?

A: It reminds us that angels are God's messengers, but Jesus is

God's Son. Prophets told about Messiah coming. Jesus is Messiah. Priests had to sacrifice every day for sin. Jesus sacrificed himself just once for all sin.

LOOKOUT FOR . . .

As you read through Hebrews, be on the lookout for . . .

Faith facts. Hebrews talks a lot about people with faith and how God responds to their faith.

Characteristics of Jesus. Hebrews talks about many different roles that Jesus fills, including priest and Savior.

God's love. In several places Hebrews reminds us that God loves and cares for us.

SPECIAL REPORT

Faith. Hebrews connects the Old Testament to the New Testament through faith in Christ. The writer of Hebrews gives many, many examples of people in the Old Testament who believed in Jesus before he even came to earth. They believed because they read in the Old Testament that Christ was coming. They were saved by trusting in God, just as people are today, because Jesus died and rose again just once for all sins of all time.

Hebrews also encourages us to have faith. As you read the New Testament, and especially Hebrews, you can look back on Christ's life just as the Old Testament believers looked forward to Christ's life. It is faith in Christ that ties the whole Bible together.

STUDY QUESTIONS

• How was Jesus a high priest? *(Hebrews 9:11-14)*

• What did God do for the people in the Old Testament who stayed faithful to him? How do we have a part in his promises? *(Hebrews 11:1-40)*

JAMES

WHY THIS BOOK?

We do not naturally thank God for trouble. Usually we do whatever we can to avoid it. But the book of James starts out with advice to let trouble "be an opportunity for joy" *(1:2)*.

The people to whom James was writing were Jewish Christians living among Gentiles. Many of them suffered for being Christians. Non-Christians would harass and mock them for it. James told his readers that these troubles could teach them to grow strong in Christ. That's why he said to be thankful for the problems.

The book of James also teaches that faith is shown by actions. A person should not just say he or she is a Christian without living like one. A Christian should want to live the way Jesus says to live. After all, God loves us so much he sent Jesus to die for us.

James also wrote that our words tell what we are like. We can ask God for wisdom, and he will help us know how to speak to others.

Another thing the book of James teaches is that we should not let a person's wealth or poverty influence our thoughts and actions toward him or her. We should be kind to all people equally.

The book of James teaches that faith and actions are both important to God.

VITAL STATS/OUTLINE

A. James' greetings *(1:1)*
James was writing to Jewish Christians everywhere.

B. Endurance *(1:2-18)*
When life is hard, faith should grow stronger, not weaker.

C. Hearing and doing the Word *(1:19–2:26)*
If we really believe what God says, we will act on it.

D. Our words and God's wisdom *(3)*
The words we speak can help a lot or hurt a lot. We need God's wisdom to control those words.

E. Trusting God *(4)*

We never know what will happen next, but we can trust God to handle it.

G. General advice on Christian living *(5)*

Do not trust money more than God. Trust him when life is difficult. Pray and love.

FAQs

Q: Does joy mean a person is laughing and singing when something really bad happens?

A: Joy is not the same thing as happiness. Happiness is usually the result of a good experience, a fun-filled time. Joy is deeper than that. It is a peace we have because we know that God is in control and he is with us no matter what happens.

Q: How can a person show faith?

A: No one can live a perfect Christian life. But a person who has faith in Jesus should be trying to live the way God said to live. A Christian should be reading God's Word and asking the Holy Spirit for help to do God's will.

LOOKOUT FOR . . .

As you read through James, be on the lookout for . . .

Direct instructions. James does not play games. He tells Christians exactly what they should do to follow God.

Evidences of faith. James tells us how to find out if our faith is true faith—by watching how we live.

Word warnings. How we use our words tells a lot about our faith.

SPECIAL REPORT

Oaths. An oath is when someone calls on God as a witness. The person is saying that God himself would say the same thing, because it is all true. In Bible times oaths were taken very seriously. There were simple oaths for everyday use and more solemn oaths for very important occasions. An example of an oath in Bible times would be someone raising his or her hand and saying "as sure as the Lord who rescues Israel lives."

An example of an everyday oath today would be when we say, "Cross my heart and hope to die if I'm not telling the truth." A more solemn oath would be when people testify in court. They have to raise their hand and sometimes put their hand on the Bible and "swear" or "promise" or "take an oath" that they are telling "the truth, the whole truth, and nothing but the truth."

James (and Jesus in his teachings) said not to take oaths. We should be truthful enough people that when we say "yes" or "no" or give some information, people know we are telling the truth. We should have a reputation for being so honest that no one needs an oath to believe what we are saying.

STUDY QUESTIONS

- How can hard times and problems be good? *(James 1:2-4)*
- What is so significant about the famous verses in *2:14-26*?
- Why is it important for us to watch what we say? *(James 3:3-12)*

1 PETER

WHY THIS BOOK?

Peter wrote this letter to Christians who were being harassed, tortured, and even threatened with their lives because of their faith. He wrote it to encourage them. They were scattered throughout Asia Minor (in modern day Turkey). But they were under pressure for believing in Jesus. Some had already been killed for their faith in Christ.

Peter spoke from experience. He himself had been beaten and put into prison because he preached about Jesus. He drew comfort from God's mercy in giving him eternal life. He also knew that taking heat for his faith strengthened it. God had promised his children eternal life with him in heaven, and that applied to him and all his Christian readers. So he told

them to expect trouble and not to fear it.

This letter was written a long time ago, but many Christians still suffer misunderstanding today. Believers in Jesus can learn from Peter how to accept it and look forward to life with Christ in heaven.

VITAL STATS/OUTLINE

A. Peter's greetings *(1:1-2)*
Peter lets them know who he is and who he is writing to.
B. Salvation *(1:3–2:3)*
God provided a way of salvation through Jesus. Because we have received that salvation we should live holy lives.

C. Do what is right *(2:4–3:12)*
Because we are Christians we have a responsibility to do what is right. That means we are to be true in our relationships.

D. Suffering *(3:13–4:19)*

Sometimes we suffer for doing what is right. We are still responsible to obey God, even when we are suffering.

E. Final advice *(5)*

Peter tells the leaders of the church to be wise and to be strong.

FAQs

Q: What good is it if Christians are persecuted for their faith?

A: If Christians live godly lives, their enemies may accuse them of doing evil, but they will glorify God in the end.

Q: Why should Christians expect suffering?

A: Christians are followers of Jesus. If he suffered, his followers will suffer too. Many people do not want to be reminded that Jesus is the only way to God.

LOOKOUT FOR . . .

As you read through 1 Peter, be on the lookout for . . .

Obeying authority. Peter talks about authority in the church as well as in the city or state.

What Christ has done for us. In many different ways, Peter tells us what Christ has done for us.

Suffering. The Christians are being harassed. This is why it is important for him to write about suffering.

SPECIAL REPORT

Persecution. "Persecution" means to harass someone or to make someone's life very difficult in any way possible. During Peter's life, the Roman emperor Nero was persecuting Christians all over the Roman empire.

The persecution happened in a lot of different ways. Sometimes Nero had Christians beaten or put in jail. Sometimes he had them killed. You may have heard some stories about Christians being put into a pen with lions and having to fight them off. Throughout history governments and people have hated Christians and have hated a God who loves them but wants them to obey. For this reason, Christians have sometimes been persecuted, but through encouragement like Peter gave, many have stood strong.

STUDY QUESTIONS

- How can Christians grow and mature? *(1 Peter 2:1-3)*
- How should Christians treat people in authority? *(1 Peter 2:13-17)*
- What should Christians do about Satan? *(1 Peter 5:8-9)*

2 PETER

WHY THIS BOOK?

The apostle Peter wrote this second letter to urge Christians to stay close to God. Peter knew that he would soon die. (He was going to be killed for his faith in Christ.) He wanted to encourage believers to continue to grow in their faith in Christ. He told them how important it was to know the Scriptures and to know Christ better and better. Peter pointed out that Scripture is God's Word and is not made up by the people who have written it down.

Peter also warned against false teachers who would come into the church after Peter was gone. He said they would deceive people and lead them into sin. Peter did not want that to happen to his brothers and sisters in Christ. Also, there would be those who denied that Jesus is coming a second time. Peter wanted believers to know that Jesus is delaying his return because God is patient and is giving people time to repent. Meanwhile, Christians should live blameless lives in peace with God and share the gospel with those around them.

2 Peter

VITAL STATS/OUTLINE

A. Greetings *(1:1)*

Peter, like Paul, states who he is (instead of just putting his name at the end of the letter).

B. Christian growth *(1:2-21)*

Scripture and faith are important ingredients of growing up.

C. False teachers *(2)*

The trouble with false teachers is that they are tricky. But God is never fooled.

D. End times *(3)*

The earth will not always keep on going just like it is. Life as we know it will change, and God will give us a new world.

FAQs

Q: What kinds of things would false teachers teach?

A: Peter warned that people calling themselves Christians will deny that Jesus is Lord. They despise authority, blaspheme, live immoral lives, teach others that immorality is OK, and boast.

Q: Why did Peter write about the world blowing up?

A: False teachers were saying that Jesus is not coming back. Peter wanted Christians to know that they were wrong. One day Jesus will return and God will create a new heaven and new earth—a new home for all his people.

LOOKOUT FOR . . .

As you read through 2 Peter, be on the lookout for . . .

The ingredients of spiritual growth. It does not happen without effort.

Characteristics of false teachers. You might notice how God will treat them.

SPECIAL REPORT

Inspiration of the Bible. Second Peter 1:20-21 is one of the most famous passages in Scripture. What it tells us is that God put his truth in Scripture. He used people to write it down. He did not tell them exactly what to write, word for word. But he did give them his truth and thoughts to write. This is called inspiration.

Inspiration is a very important doctrine (belief) in the Christian faith. It means that the Bible is different from every other book in the world because God himself created it. Songwriters and authors talk about being inspired, but that is different—it means that they have a great idea and they are not sure where it came from. The Bible is inspired by God himself. Because of that, we need to read it, learn it, and obey it.

STUDY QUESTIONS

- Where did Scripture come from? (2 Peter 1:20-21)
- How does God see time? (2 Peter 3:8-9)
- Since judgment is coming, how should Christians live? (2 Peter 3:11-13)

1 JOHN

WHY THIS BOOK?

Why do people like
eyewitness news? They want to
know the facts. They do not want
to play the game "Telephone" or
"Gossip" when it comes to
important matters.

The apostle John was an
eyewitness to the life of Jesus. He
had been there when Jesus was
living on earth. He had heard Jesus
with his own ears. He had seen
Jesus with his own eyes. He had
worked alongside Jesus with his
own hands. John knew Jesus
personally. He knew all about
Jesus and he knew the truth about
Jesus.

John wrote about this
because some people were
teaching that Jesus was not really
God in the flesh. They said that Jesus
was more like a ghost than a real human being. They also said that it
did not matter what people do with their bodies since they will die
anyway. Their ideas were making Christians wonder if it was OK to
sin.

John wanted Christians to know that Jesus is real and really gave them eternal life. John wanted them to know that anyone born into God's family does not make sin a way of life. But when Christians do sin, they can ask Jesus to forgive them. He does forgive people when they repent, and they can have fellowship with God and with each other. That is the truth about Jesus.

VITAL STATS/OUTLINE

A. Jesus is life and light *(1)*
His life lives within us and his light shows us our sin.
B. Love one another and do not sin *(2:1–3:24)*
When we do not love, we are sinning, because God is love.
C. False prophets *(4:1-6)*
A prophet is false who does not acknowledge Jesus as the Son of God.
D. The love of God in us *(4:7-21)*
God loves us, and that is why we should love each other.
E. Believe in Jesus *(5)*
God gives us life through his son.

FAQs

Q: Just because John knew Jesus was a person, how did he know that Jesus was God too?

A: John was with Peter and James when Jesus was transfigured. They saw Jesus' divine glory. They also heard God the Father say that Jesus is his Son.

Q: How did John say people should love their neighbors?

A: John said love is not just words but also actions. For instance, he said if a Christian friend needs food or clothing, it is not enough to say, "I hope you find food or clothing." You should give the person food or clothing. Christian love gives help to people in need.

LOOKOUT FOR . . .

As you read through 1 John, be on the lookout for . . .

Love. John's love for his readers, God's love for us, our love for each other.

Sin. Its presence and what it causes in our lives.

SPECIAL REPORT

Antichrist. The word "antichrist" refers to any enemy of Jesus Christ or someone who tries to take away Jesus' power. The word appears in

some versions of the Bible only a few times. But the meaning of this word appears throughout the Bible.

Both the Old and New Testament talk about a person or a power at the end of time who will attack God's people and try to take God's place. This is described in Ezekiel 38–39, Psalm 2, Zechariah 12–14, and 2 Thessalonians 2:1-12, as well as others.

John uses the word "antichrist" in two ways. In chapter four he talks about the antichrist who will come at the end of time. He also uses the word in chapter two to talk about anyone who tries to tear down the work of Christ. John did this so that his friends would beware of all antichrists and stay away from them.

STUDY QUESTIONS

- What should a Christian do when he or she sins? *(1 John 1:9)*
- What does "love the world" mean? *(1 John 2:15-17)*
- What does John say Christians will be like when Jesus returns? *(1 John 3:1-3)*

2 JOHN

WHY THIS BOOK?

The shortest book in the Bible can be summed up in two words: Truth and Love.

The apostle John wrote this short note called 2 John. He warned his dear friend in Christ to beware of those who were not teaching the truth. This special lady probably opened her home to traveling preachers. She was trying to show Christian love and hospitality. But John warned her that not all the teachers and preachers were telling the truth.

There were those who taught that Jesus was not really a human being. They denied the truth of Jesus Christ as God and man. They were teaching a wrong idea. If the lady welcomed them, others would think the teachers were good to listen to. Many people would be confused. If people believe in a Jesus who is not the true Jesus, then they are not really trusting God.

VITAL STATS/OUTLINE

A. Greetings *(1:1-3)*
Greets a lady, but this may mean a church.

B. Remain faithful *(1:4-6)*
Continue to love each other.
C. Beware of false teachers *(1:7-13)*
Be careful about people who teach lies.

FAQs

Q: Why did John tell us not to invite people into our homes when we're supposed to show hospitality?

A: John was not saying that we should keep non-Christians out of our homes. But he did not want people who were teaching wrong ideas about Jesus to be held up as leaders whom people should follow. These false teachers could cause many people to miss the truth.

Q: Are there false teachers today?

A: Many people today teach that Jesus was just a good man. They say he was not really God. But the Bible teaches that he is both God and man.

Q: Why is it important that Jesus is God and man?

A: Two reasons. First, only God is good enough to pay the debt for our sin. Second, he needed to be a human so he could show us how to live in God's family here on earth. Jesus is a bridge between us and the Heavenly Father.

LOOKOUT FOR . . .

As you read through 2 John, be on the lookout for . . .

Love. John always encourages his readers to love one another.

Strong warnings. John is almost harsh when he talks about false teachers.

SPECIAL REPORT

Gnostics. False doctrine means wrong ideas about God. John wrote 2 John to guard against the wrong idea that it does not matter how we live our lives, as long as God has saved us. This wrong idea, or lie, was held by a group of people called the Gnostics (pronounced "nah-sticks").

Part of the reason John wrote this letter was to remind us that it does matter how we live our lives. God has commanded us to love, and that is what we should do.

STUDY QUESTIONS

• What is God's definition of love? (*2 John 1:6*)
• Why is 2 John so short? (*2 John 1:12*)

3 JOHN

WHY THIS BOOK?

There were no big fancy hotels when the apostle John lived. Instead, traveling teachers and missionaries stayed in homes of other Christians. One of those Christians was John's friend Gaius.

The apostle John wrote this short letter to Gaius. John was glad to know that Gaius was being faithful to Christ. Gaius was sharing his home and things with the traveling preachers. It was important to John that Christians helped their fellow Christians in the ministry. John did not want the missionaries to be in need.

Giving the missionaries food and a place to rest was a way for the believers to be partners in ministry.

Another man in the church was refusing to help the missionaries. His name was Diotrephes. He also would not let anyone else help them. John told Gaius not to follow Diotrephes' bad example.

VITAL STATS/OUTLINE

A. Greetings *(1:1-2)*
From John, to Gaius.
B. Good job! *(1:3-8)*
Gaius has been very hospitable to traveling preachers.
C. Diotrephes *(1:9-10)*
Diotrephes is saying bad things about the apostles and is causing trouble in the church.
D. Choose good examples *(1:11-15)*
Demetrius is trustworthy and a good example for Gaius to follow.

FAQs

Q: Why did John warn "the chosen lady" in 2 John but say nice things about Gaius in 3 John?

A: The people in 2 John were teaching false doctrines. John did not want anyone to be confused by their lies. In the case of 3 John, the traveling preachers were teaching the truth. John wanted the believers to encourage and help them as much as they could.

Q: Why didn't John want the pagans to help the missionaries?

A: John didn't want nonbelievers to think the missionaries and teachers were just trying to get money for themselves.

Q: How should Christians help missionaries today?

A: Believers can share their homes with visiting missionaries just as Gaius did. Eating meals together is a great way to get to know people. Knowing people helps us pray for them better. It helps us find out other ways we can help them in their ministry. And missionaries' children need friends when they come to town—local Christian kids who can be their friends.

LOOKOUT FOR . . .

As you read through 3 John, be on the lookout for . . .

Good examples. John mentions a bad example and a good example. What is the difference between the two?

Hospitality. John compliments Gaius on hosting traveling preachers and missionaries.

SPECIAL REPORT

Bad examples. Diotrephes might not have acted so badly if he had known that the whole world would learn about it. We do not know exactly why Diotrephes refused to take care of the traveling Christians the way Gaius did, but the Scripture says, "Diotrephes, who loves to be the leader, . . . " and that gives us a hint.

It might have been that Diotrephes was jealous of other leaders. It might have been that he wanted to be the important one, and when other guests arrived he was afraid he would not seem so important. For whatever reason, Diotrephes was a bad example. He is an example of a person who was unkind to others who got more attention than he did.

STUDY QUESTIONS

• How did John show that our bodies and our spirits are important to God? (3 John 1:2)

• What is something that gave John joy? (Hint: It would probably give your parents joy too!) (3 John 1:4)

JUDE

WHY THIS BOOK?

Ever since the beginning of the church, Christians have had to beware of false teachers. Jude wrote this book to warn believers that false teaching could lead to sad consequences.

Jude was a brother of James and a half brother of Jesus. Like James, at first he did not believe that Jesus was the Messiah. But after Jesus rose from the dead, Jude believed.

Jude's main concern was false teachers. They were saying that Christians can do whatever they want because of God's grace. They taught that they did not have to obey any authority.

Instead, Jude reminded the Christians to stay close to Christ, to love and obey him. He also said they should help others understand God's truth so they could be saved too.

Jude was not trying to scare anybody. He closed his letter with the great promise that Jesus is able to keep us from falling. He praised the Savior for his majesty, power, and authority!

VITAL STATS/OUTLINE

A. Greetings *(1:1-2)*
Jude greets all Christians.
B. False teachers *(1:3-19)*
Jude reminds his readers that God hated sin in the past and still does.
C. Strong faith *(1:20-25)*
Jude encourages Christians to stick to what they know is right no matter what.

FAQs

Q: Why did Jude warn Christians about false teachers?

A: What we think about God is very important. As Jude pointed out, consider the angels who followed Satan and

rebelled against God. They believed a false teacher, Satan. The same thing happened among the people of Sodom and Gomorrah, cities filled with people who did not care about God. Cain, Balaam, and Korah all suffered because they followed wrong ideas about God.

Q: Doesn't the Bible teach that God will forgive any sin?

A: God does forgive any sin. But he does not want people to live in sin. He wants us to turn to him and trust in Jesus Christ. Then he gives us power to turn from our sin.

LOOKOUT FOR . . .

As you read through Jude, be on the lookout for . . .

Punishment of sin. Jude spends a great deal of time telling about sinful people and how God punished them.

The Christian life. Jude closes with a great description of the Christian life.

SPECIAL REPORT

Sodom and Gomorrah. Jude refers to an Old Testament story about two towns, Sodom and Gomorrah. The story is found in

Genesis 18 and 19. God told Abraham that he was going to destroy these towns because of their wickedness. Abraham's nephew, Lot, lived there. Abraham asked God to spare the cities if only he could find ten righteous people there. But he could not even find ten.

God told them not to look back as they left. The town burned to the ground. Unfortunately Lot's wife disobeyed God and looked back at her burning home and turned into a pillar of salt.

To this day, just as in Jude's day, Sodom and Gomorrah remind us of God's judgment of sin.

STUDY QUESTION

• How will it be when we see the Lord? (*Jude 1:24-25*)

REVELATION

WHY THIS BOOK?

Sometimes Christians become discouraged by sin and evil in the world. A good remedy is to read the book of Revelation—especially the last four chapters. Then you may feel like the man who cheered and hollered, "Yea! I read the end of the book! We win!"

Revelation is the only book of prophecy in the New Testament. It is also called the Apocalypse. There are promises of blessing to those who read, hear, and keep the words of Revelation. The apostle John wrote Revelation when he was very old. He was an exile on the island of Patmos because he refused to stop preaching about Jesus.

Jesus gave John this vision to tell Christians what was going to happen. Jesus gave special messages to seven different churches that were in Asia. Jesus commended the churches for their strengths and scolded them for their failings. Then he gave instructions for what they could do to correct the problems. These same problems exist today. Christians can learn from Jesus' words to the churches.

The book of Revelation is filled with symbolic language. It tells how unbelievers will fight against Jesus and God's people. It urges believers to stay true to Jesus and not to believe Satan's lies. And in the end, it tells of Christ's great victory.

The joy of being with Jesus in heaven for all eternity far outweighs the difficulties we will have on earth.

VITAL STATS/OUTLINE

A. Jesus is coming back *(1)*
John describes his vision of Jesus returning.
B. Seven letters to seven churches *(2–3)*
John writes to seven specific churches telling them good things and bad things about the way they are serving God.
C. Vision of the end of earth as it is now *(4–19)*
John's visions include scrolls, trumpets, creatures we have never seen, angels, plagues, a wedding banquet, and horses.

D. The end of time (20–22)
Satan's final punishment, the new earth, and the new heaven.

FAQs

Q: What were the things Jesus commended the churches for?

A: Jesus commended the churches for hard work, suffering persecution and poverty, being true to faith, for love and service, and for being effective.

Q: What things did they do that he didn't like?

A: Jesus rebuked the churches for forgetting their first love, for compromising, for immorality, for being superficial, and for being lukewarm. Two churches were not scolded at all. The churches at Smyrna and Philadelphia got nothing but A-pluses from Jesus.

LOOKOUT FOR . . .

As you read through Revelation, be on the lookout for . . .

Messages to the churches. There are seven messages for seven specific churches.

Signs of the times. John gives us many clues to what will happen when Christ comes back and sets up his new kingdom.

SPECIAL REPORT

Visions. John describes heavenly events by comparing them to things we have seen on earth. These are called his visions. There are many visions listed in the Bible. In Genesis 28:10-14 Jacob sees a vision of angels going up and down a stairway that leads into heaven. Ezekiel saw many visions. In the first chapter of his book, he describes a vision of a windstorm and creatures that looked like men with wings and with feet like calves. Daniel also had many visions. Some of both Ezekiel's and Daniel's visions had to do with the last days of the earth just as John's did. These are called apocalyptic visions.

Revelation describes visions of horses and riders and much more. It has many visions. And each one describes something that will happen in the future. These visions give us a glimpse into the future, but when it all really happens it will be like nothing we have ever seen before.

STUDY QUESTIONS

• What awful punishment awaits those who worship the beast? *(Revelation 14:9-11)*

• What will eternity with God be like? *(Revelation 21:1–22:7)*

APPENDIX

BIG IDEAS IN THE BIBLE

Hey, what's the big idea? Actually, the Bible has several big ideas. Think of them as words, phrases, and ideas that you need to know if you want to understand the Bible.

Ascension: Jesus' return to heaven after his death and resurrection.

Assembly: A gathering of God's people for worship; another word for congregation.

Atonement: Payment for sin. Jesus' death made atonement for all our sins.

Baptism: A sign that a person is a follower of Christ. Some churches pour water over the person's head, others dip the person all the way down under the water. Some churches only baptize people old enough to understand baptism. Some churches baptize babies when their parents ask for it.

Beatitudes: A word meaning "blessings"; part of Jesus' Sermon on the Mount describes what makes people blessed.

Birthright: The legal right to be the leader of the family and to get a double amount of the inheritance when the father dies. Jacob traded a bowl of stew for Esau's birthright.

Bless: To pray God's best for someone; to wish the person well; to speak well of the person.

Book of Life: The record of those who trust in Christ and will live in heaven with him.

Born again: To be born spiritually by trusting in Christ's death and resurrection; the work of the Holy Spirit which saves a person.

Church: All true believers in Christ; a group of Christians.

Confess: To admit your sins; to say publicly what you believe.

Covenant: A promise or agreement between two or more people. God made a covenant with Abraham. God promised to bless the whole world through Abraham's descendants.

Cross: The place where the Romans executed Jesus; a symbol of Jesus' great love and sacrifice in taking away our sins.

Curse: To wish or speak harm on someone; to damn; the opposite of bless. Jesus said to curse someone is as bad as murder.

Dedicate: To set something aside for God. Hannah dedicated Samuel to God before he was born.

Depraved: Unable to be good enough for God. Only Jesus can change people and give them a new nature.

Divination: Trying to tell the future by using astrology, magic, witchcraft, or some other occult power. God forbids divination (Deuteronomy 18:10-11).

Eternal life: The new life Jesus gives people when they trust in him as Savior. Eternal life begins immediately and goes on through eternity.

Faith: Complete trust in God that he exists and what he said in the Bible is true—even though he is invisible. Obeying him.

Fear of the Lord: Respect for God and his authority.

Forgive: To pardon or cancel a debt; to wipe the record clean. When people place their trust in Jesus, God forgives their sin.

Fruit of the Spirit: The result in a people's lives whenever they let the Holy Spirit have control. The fruit is love, joy, peace, patience, kindness, goodness, faithfulness, gentleness, and self-control (Galatians 5:22-23).

Glorification: The promise that Christians will be like Jesus when he takes them home to heaven (1 John 3:2-3).

Grace: God's free gift of forgiveness and salvation; kindness; favor.

Holiness: Purity; being completely without sin. God is holy.

Justification: God seeing us as sinless even though we are not. He does this for every person who trusts in Jesus.

Mercy: God's goodness to us even though we do not deserve it.

Redemption: The work that Jesus did on the cross; he paid the debt for our sin.

Repentance: Turning away from sin and turning toward God.

Resurrection: Coming alive from death. Jesus rose three days after he was crucified. Believers who die before Jesus returns will be resurrected at his second coming.

Salvation: God's free gift of forgiveness from sin and a new life in Christ. Everyone is a sinner, but Christ's death on the cross paid the penalty for our sin. Each person who trusts in Christ for forgiveness receives salvation.

Sin: Going against God's will; disobeying God; doing wrong. Every person sins.

Soul, spirit: The emotions, mind, and personality of a person; what lives on after the body dies.

Temptation: Wanting to do wrong, to sin.

Unbelief: Refusing to believe God or his Word; the opposite of faith.

Big Ideas

Wisdom: Understanding; insight; prone to make good choices. The book of Proverbs urges us to seek wisdom from God.

Zeal: Strong devotion to a cause or person.

PROMISES IN THE BIBLE

Promises Made to Believers

An abundant life
John 10:10

A crown of life
Revelation 2:10

A home in heaven
John 14:1-3

Answered prayer
1 John 5:14

Assurances for the future
2 Timothy 1:12

Cleansing
John 15:3

Comfort
Isaiah 51:3

God's deliverance
2 Timothy 4:18

Everlasting life
John 3:16

Promises in the Bible

Fellowship with Christ
Matthew 18:19

Gifts of the Spirit
1 Corinthians 12

God's care
1 Peter 5:6-7

Growth in the Christian life
Ephesians 4:11-15

God's guidance
Isaiah 42:16

Hope
Hebrews 6:18-19

Christian's inheritance
1 Peter 1:3-4

Joy
Isaiah 35:10

Peace
John 14:27

Rest
Hebrews 4:9, 11

Resurrection
Romans 8:11

Spiritual healing
Hosea 6:1

Spiritual light
John 12:46

Strength
Philippians 4:13

Understanding
Psalm 119:104

Victory
1 John 5:4

Wisdom
James 1:5

FIFTY VERY IMPORTANT PASSAGES

The Bible is a very big book. Here are some of the most important passages you will ever read in it.

The Creation	*Genesis 1*
The First Sin	*Genesis 3*
Noah and the Flood	*Genesis 6–9:17*
The Tower of Babel	*Genesis 11:1-9*
Abraham and Isaac	*Genesis 22:1-19*
Esau and Jacob	*Genesis 25:19-34; 27*
The Life of Joseph	*Genesis 37–50*
Baby Moses	*Exodus 2:1-10*
God Frees the Israelites	*Exodus 7–14*
The Ten Commandments	*Exodus 20*
Jericho Is Captured	*Joshua 6:15-21*
Gideon's Little Army	*Judges 7:15-23*
The Life of Samson	*Judges 13–16*
Story of Ruth	*Book of Ruth*
The Boy Samuel	*1 Samuel 1–3*
David Kills Goliath	*1 Samuel 17*
The Shepherd Psalm	*Psalm 23*
The Fiery Furnace	*Daniel 3*
Daniel in the Lions' Den	*Daniel 6*
Story of Jonah	*Book of Jonah*
The Birth of Jesus	*Luke 2*
John the Baptist Preaches	*Matthew 3:1-12*
Young Jesus in the Temple	*Luke 2:41-52*
The Baptism of Jesus	*Matthew 3:13-17; John 1:31-34*
Jesus Is Tempted	*Matthew 4:1-11; Luke 4:1-11*

The Sermon on the Mount	*Matthew 5–7*
The Lord's Prayer	*Matthew 6:9–13; Luke 11:2-4*
The Woman at the Well	*John 4:1-42*
Becoming Fishers of Men	*Matthew 4:18-22; Luke 5:1-11*
The Centurion's Faith	*Luke 7:1-10; John 4:43-54*
The Story of the Sower	*Matthew 13:1-23; Mark 4:1-20*
The True Vine	*John 15*
The Prodigal Son	*Luke 15:11-32*
Jesus' Transfiguration	*Matthew 17:1-13; Mark 9:2-13*
Mary and Martha	*Luke 10:38-42*
Zacchaeus	*Luke 19:1-10*
Mary Anoints Jesus	*Mark 14:3-9; John 12:1-8*
The Last Supper	*Matthew 26:17-30; Mark 14:12-26*
Jesus Is Betrayed	*Mark 14:10-11; Luke 22:1-6; John 18:1-11*
Death & Resurrection of Jesus	*Matthew 27–28; Mark 15–16; Luke 23–24:2; John 19:16–20:10*
The Risen Christ	*Luke 24:35–49; John 20:19-23*
Doubting Thomas	*John 20:24-29*
The Great Commission	*Matthew 28:16-20*
The Holy Spirit Comes	*Acts 2*
Conversion of Saul	*Acts 9:1-9*
Peter Is Rescued from Prison	*Acts 12:1-19*
Paul's Missionary Travels	*Acts 13-21*
Living for God	*Romans 12*
Love	*1 Corinthians 13*
The Future	*Revelation 21:1-8*

HOW THE BIBLE IS ORGANIZED

- *Why is the Bible set up the way it is?*
- *How did Genesis get to be first?*
- *Why does Luke come after Malachi?*

The Bible really does have an order to it. Each book belongs to a category. Here is how it is all laid out, from beginning to end.

Books of Law
These five books tell the story of how God gave us his law:
Genesis, Exodus, Leviticus, Numbers, Deuteronomy

Books of History
These books tell about the history of God's people Israel:
Joshua, Judges, Ruth, 1 Samuel, 2 Samuel, 1 Kings, 2 Kings, 1 Chronicles, 2 Chronicles, Ezra, Nehemiah, Esther

Books of Poetry
These five books have almost all poetry in them:
Job, Psalms, Proverbs, Ecclesiastes, Song of Songs

Major Prophets
These books record the prophecies of God's most well-known prophets:
Isaiah, Jeremiah, Lamentations, Ezekiel, Daniel

Minor Prophets
These books record the prophecies of God's less well-known

prophets:

Hosea, Joel, Amos, Obadiah, Jonah, Micah, Nahum, Habakkuk, Zephaniah, Haggai, Zechariah, Malachi

Gospels

These books tell the Good News about Jesus:
Matthew, Mark, Luke, John, Acts

Letters of Paul

These books are letters that the apostle Paul wrote:
Romans, 1 Corinthians, 2 Corinthians, Galatians, Ephesians, Philippians, Colossians, 1 Thessalonians, 2 Thessalonians, 1 Timothy, 2 Timothy, Titus, Philemon

General Letters

These books are all the letters in the New Testament that Paul did not write:
Hebrews, James, 1 Peter, 2 Peter, 1 John, 2 John, 3 John, Jude

New Testament Prophecy

This book is the New Testament's lone book of prophecy:
Revelation

FAMOUS PRAYERS

Most people would expect to find prayers in the Bible. But not everyone would know where to find some of them. Here are some of the prayers that played a key part in God's work.

Abraham's prayer for an heir
Genesis 15:2-3

Isacc's prayer for Jacob and Esau
Genesis 25:21-23

Hannah's prayer for a son
1 Samuel 1:9-13

Abraham's prayer for Sodom
Genesis 18:23-33

Christians' prayer for Peter's safety
Acts 12:5

Moses' prayer for God to send plagues on Egypt
Exodus 8-12

Moses' prayer for God to part the waters of the Red Sea
Exodus 14:21

Joshua's prayer for more sunlight
Joshua 10:12

Gideon's prayer for a sign from God
Judges 6:36-40

Samson's prayer for strength
Judges 16:28-31

Samson's prayer for wisdom
1 Kings 3:5-9

David's prayers of praise
Psalms 100, 103, 106, 107

Prayer of praise for the Red Sea deliverance
Exodus 15

David's prayer for forgiveness
Psalm 32, 51

Elijah's prayer for fire
1 Kings 18:36-37

Daniel's prayer to interpret a dream
Daniel 2:18

Stephen's prayer on the behalf of his killers
Acts 7:59-60

Church's prayer for missionaries
Acts 13:3

Famous Prayers

Mary and Martha's prayer for their sick brother
John 11:30

Elijah's prayer for a dead boy
1 Kings 17:20-21

Elisha's prayer for a dead son
2 Kings 4:33-35

Peter's prayer for Dorcas
Acts 9:36-43

Hannah's prayer for praise for the birth of Samuel
1 Samuel 2:1-10

Anna and Simeon thank God for Christ
Luke 2:25-38

Mary's prayer of thanks for being his handmaiden
Luke 1:46-55

David thanks God for his great mercy
Psalm 136

Job's prayer because of his suffering
Job 3:3-12; 10:18-22

Jonah's prayer because God spared Nineveh
Jonah 4

Thanking God for salvation
Revelation 5:8-14; 7:9-12

THE MIRACLES OF JESUS

The first miracle that Jesus did was at a wedding in Cana when he turned water into wine. After that he did many more miracles and became more and more well-known. Following is a list of Jesus' miracles which are recorded in the Bible.

Changing water to wine
John 2:7-9

Healing rich man's son
John 4:50

Healing of demoniac
Mark 1:25; Luke 4:35

Healing Peter's mother-in-law
Matthew 8:15; Mark 1:31; Luke 4:39

Catching many fish
Luke 5:5-6

Healing a leper
Matthew 8:3; Mark 1:41

Healing a paralytic
Matthew 9:2, 6, 7; Mark 2:5, 10-12; Luke 5:20, 24, 25

Healing a withered hand
Matthew 12:13; Mark 3:5; Luke 6:10

Healing centurion's servant
Matthew 8:13; Luke 7:10

Raising a widow's son
Luke 7:14

Calming a stormy sea
Matthew 8:26; Mark 4:39; Luke 8:24

Healing Gadarene demoniac
Matthew 8:32; Mark 5:8; Luke 8:33

Healing a bleeding woman
Matthew 9:22; Mark 5:29; Luke 8:44

Raising Jairus' daughter
Matthew 9:25; Mark 5:41; Luke 8:54

Healing two blind men
Matthew 9:29

Healing dumb demoniac
Matthew 9:33

Healing invalid
John 5:8

Miracles of Jesus

Feeding of 5,000
Matthew 14:19; Mark 6:41; Luke 9:16; John 6:11

Walking on the water
Matthw 14:25; Mark 6:48; John 6:19

Healing of demon-possessed girl
Matthew 15:28; Mark 7:29

Healing of deaf man
Mark 7:34, 35

Feeding of 4,000
Mark 15:36; Mark 8:6

Healing a blind man
Mark 8:25

Healing man who was born blind
John 9:7

Healing demoniac boy
Matthew 17:18; Mark 9:25; Luke 9:42

Catching a fish with coin in it's mouth
Matthew 17:27

Healing a blind and dumb demoniac
Matthew 12:22; Luke 11:14

Healing woman who had been sick for 18 years
Luke 13:10-17

Healing man with dropsy
Luke 14:4

Healing ten lepers
Luke 17:11-19

Raising of Lazarus
John 11:43, 44

Healing blind man
Matthew 20:34; Luke 18:42

Destroying fig tree
Matthew 21:19; Mark 11:14

Healing the severed ear
Matthew 26:51; Mark 14:47; Luke 22:50, 51; John 18:10

Catching a great number of fish
John 21:6

LIFE AND TIMES OF JESUS

Jesus is the main person of the whole Bible. In the very first book of the Bible, God said someone would crush Satan. It was the first promise of a Savior. Later, all through the Old Testament, God's messengers, the prophets, told of someone who would come to make things right.

The New Testament is all about that Savior, Jesus Christ. It tells about his birth, life, teachings, miracles, death, and resurrection. It also tells about his followers and how they spread the Good News about Jesus the Savior.

What Child Is This?

Jesus came into the world like no other child before him. A young Jewish woman named Mary was engaged to be married to a carpenter named Joseph. Mary was a virgin. Then God's Holy Spirit made Mary pregnant. Joseph was not the father at all—God was. Centuries before Jesus was born, God's messengers had said that's how it would happen. Jesus would be the Son of God and the Son of Man at the same time.

An angel told Mary she would have God's special baby. Later, an angel told Joseph that Mary was pregnant by the Spirit of God, and that Joseph should still marry her. And when Jesus was born, angels announced his birth to shepherds late at night. God sent a special star to guide wise men to the new king of the Jews. Two old people named Simeon and Anna, who loved God, recognized the baby Jesus as the Savior God had promised long ago.

Joseph was a carpenter and Jesus learned his earthly father's trade. Joseph and Mary had other children who were Jesus' half brothers and sisters. They lived in Nazareth. In most ways, their family was like any other ordinary Jewish family in Nazareth.

When Jesus was 12 years old, he went to Jerusalem with his parents for a special holiday called Passover. Later they found him talking with the teachers. Everyone was amazed at how much he understood and knew.

For many years, Jesus worked as a carpenter. He probably seemed very ordinary. But when he was about 33 years old, things changed.

Look! The Lamb of God

Jesus had a cousin named John. John was called the Baptizer because he was baptizing people. John was preparing the way for the Messiah. When Jesus went to John to be baptized, John heard God say to Jesus, "You are my beloved Son, and I am fully pleased with you" (Luke 3:22).

After that, Jesus spent time in the desert where he prayed and didn't eat anything for 40 days. Satan tempted Jesus. He tried to get Jesus to worship him and to turn his back on God the Father. But Jesus stood firm against the Devil. Jesus was ready to do the work God sent him to do.

The Teacher

Jesus began teaching people about God. The religious leaders had made many extra rules about how to worship God. They made it so hard for people to know God that many people just went through the motions of keeping the laws. Other people gave up completely.

Many people liked to listen to Jesus. Crowds followed him from town to town as he taught about God's love and hope. Jesus always spent a lot of time praying to the Father. One day after praying, he chose 12 men from the crowd of people to be his disciples. The men left their jobs. For three years they lived and traveled with Jesus. They listened to his messages, watched his miracles, and asked questions about everything they didn't understand. He told them he was going to die and rise again. But they didn't understand all that he said until after Jesus' death and resurrection.

Jesus talked to the people in parables—stories that he took from everyday life. He told them what God's kingdom is like. He said his followers love their enemies and serve each other. He taught about God's love for people. He talked about forgiveness, purity, faithfulness in marriage, honesty, keeping promises, obeying God, getting rid of sin, being thankful, and many other things.

The Healer

Talking wasn't all that Jesus did. Jesus showed his love and his power by healing people who were blind, unable to walk, unable to talk, and who had other serious diseases. He fed large crowds of people (more than 5,000 at one time) with a few fish and loaves of bread. He cast demons out of people. He even brought dead people back to life, including a little girl, a young man, and a grown man.

The Friend

Something else special about Jesus was the way he treated women and children. In his day, they were almost like property. Jesus didn't treat them that way. He was respectful and kind to women and children. He said people had to become like children in order to enter God's kingdom. When he was on the cross, he made sure someone would take care of his dear mother.

But Jesus didn't get along with everyone. He scolded the

religious leaders for thinking they were better than others. They didn't think they needed a Savior. They, in turn, didn't like Jesus because he called God his father and he spent time with people who were not very "religious." It was the religious leaders who grew to hate Jesus so much they had him crucified.

God's Plan

Actually, Jesus was born to die. God had planned it before time. Jesus left his throne in heaven with the purpose of making a way for people to be in God's family. Jesus was the only human being good enough to die for the sins of the world. Because he is God, he is perfect and sinless. He became a man so he could show people how to live. He died on the cross to pay the penalty for all the sins of all people in all time.

When it came time for Jesus to die, it was one of his own disciples who betrayed him. Another one denied even knowing him. The rest of the disciples ran away. Jesus knew all this was going to happen. In fact, the night before, he prayed and asked the Father to protect his disciples. Jesus also prayed for all the people who would believe in him in the future.

Jesus' Death

Jesus was arrested at night and taken to an illegal trial. He had done nothing wrong so there was no evidence against him. But he was beaten and mocked and treated like a criminal. Pilate, the Roman ruler, wanted to let him go. But the religious leaders led the crowd in calling for him to be crucified. Pilate didn't want the people to riot, so he gave in.

Crucifixion was a painful, shameful death. In addition to the physical pain Jesus experienced, he felt all the sin and guilt of all the people in the world for all time on him. God the Father actually turned away from his beloved Son because of the sin. It was such a horrible thing, that the sky grew dark and the heavy curtain in the Temple tore from top to bottom.

All the men had deserted Jesus. Only the women who loved and followed him and helped support his ministry stayed at the cross until he died. Then two men who had been secret believers in Jesus asked Pilate for his body. They buried him in a cave while the women watched.

Alive Again!

But on the third day, early Sunday morning, some of the women went to put spices on the body. It was their way of showing care and respect for the dead. To their complete surprise, the tomb was empty and an angel said that Jesus had risen, just as he had said he would!

The women ran back to the house where the other disciples were. They tried to tell them the Good News about Jesus. No one would believe them at first. It wasn't till Jesus appeared in the middle of the room without going through the door that they believed.

Jesus appeared to all the disciples at different times as well as to 500 other believers before he returned to heaven to make a place for his people to live for eternity. He promised to return someday and to take them to be with him in heaven. No one knows when that will happen. He has kept all his promises so far. He will surely keep this promise as well.

OLD TESTAMENT TIMELINE

Approximate dates

All dates are B.C.

0	God Creates Everything
3000-2500	Noah and the Great Flood
2400	Tower of Babel
2066	Birth of Isaac
1900	Destruction of Sodom and Gomorrah
1800	Joseph Sold into Slavery
1500	Birth of Moses
1470	Israel Escapes through the Red Sea
1440	God Gives Moses the Ten Commandments
1400	Joshua Captures Jericho
1100	Samson Is the Strongest Man
1009	David Becomes King of Judah
975	Solomon Builds the Temple
870	Elijah Lives and Prophesies
775	Jonah Obeys God
626	Jeremiah Lives and Writes
621	Book of God's Law Found
600	Daniel Explains Nebuchadnezzar's Dream
584	Shadrach, Meshach, Abednego in the Fiery Furnace
541	Daniel in the Lions' Den
480	Esther Saves the Jews
444	Walls of Jerusalem Rebuilt
135	Rome Rules the Jews

NEW TESTAMENT TIMELINE

Dates are approximate

37 B.C.	Herod Becomes King of Judea
3	Jesus Is Born
1	Wise Men Worship Jesus
1	Mary, Joseph and Jesus Escape to Egypt
27–30 A.D.	Jesus Ministers and Performs Miracles
30	Jesus Is Crucified
30	God Sends the Holy Spirit
32	Stephen Is Martyred
32	Paul Is Converted to Christianity
34–38	Gentiles Become Christians
45–47	Paul's First Missionary Journey
50–90	Letters Written to Churches
58	Paul Imprisoned
60	Paul's Trip to Rome
60–63	Paul Imprisoned at Home
64	Paul and Peter Martyred
95	Jesus' Reveals Future to John

WHAT'S IN THE OLD TESTAMENT

The Old Testament is 39 books of all shapes and sizes. From the first book, Genesis, to the last book, Malachi, almost every book is different. Some books tell a story about specific people. Some give lists of rules and regulations. Some are poems. Some are sermons. God used all different kinds of people and all different kinds of writing to put together the Old Testament. He did this so that we would know how we were created. He also did this to show how he has offered his friendship to us through the many years before he came to earth as Jesus Christ to talk with us directly.

Even though Jesus is not mentioned by name in the Old Testament, the Old Testament is about Jesus in many ways. In the Old Testament God was teaching his people to believe that Christ would come to earth. That's why the Old Testament is full of sacrifices and promises of freedom. That was what Christ was coming to do—offer his life as a sacrifice and set people free from sin. The Old Testament makes many prophecies or predictions about Christ that came true in the New Testament.

In the Beginning . . .

The Old Testament starts with the story of God's creation of the world, including people, with Adam and Eve in the Garden of Eden. By the time Noah is raising his family, though, God cannot find more than a handful of righteous people on earth. After Noah is saved from the Flood in a huge boat, God starts over again with Noah and his three sons. From one of those sons comes Abraham. God makes a special agreement, called a covenant, with Abraham. He promises that Abraham will have a big family and that they will have a special relationship with God if they follow his laws. Abraham's family and descendants were called Hebrews or Israelites. Today they are called Jews.

Spotlight on the Jews

The rest of the Old Testament is about that family. They grow to be a whole nation of people. They are held captive in Egypt, but they get away because of miracles God performs through Moses. They wander through the desert back to their homeland, Israel. They win wars and lose wars. They obey God and then they disobey him. The last part of the Old Testament is sermons by the prophets of the Hebrews reminding them to obey God. The prophets reminded them that their lives were always better when they followed God's way of doing things.

Books of the Law

The first five books of the Old Testament, Genesis, Exodus, Leviticus, Numbers, and Deuteronomy, are called the books of the law. Genesis tells about the beginnings of the world and the beginnings of the Jewish nation. Exodus tells about the Hebrews leaving Egypt and wandering in the desert. Leviticus is a list of their rules for living. Numbers is a list of who they all were and how many were in each of the twelve families. Deuteronomy is a book made up of Moses' words to his people before he died. It tells them how to follow God.

Books of History

There are twelve books in the Old Testament called history books: Joshua, Judges, Ruth, 1 and 2 Samuel, 1 and 2 Kings, 1 and 2

Chronicles, Ezra, Nehemiah, and Esther. There are other books besides these that mention facts of history, but these books specifically tell the story of history. Joshua tells the story of the Hebrews after Moses died. Judges tells about wise men and women that ruled Israel. Ruth tells the story of one Jewish lady in particular who came back home to Bethlehem. 1 and 2 Samuel, 1 and 2 Kings, and 1 and 2 Chronicles tell the stories of the Jewish nation and all it's kings and courts and armies. Ezra and Nehemiah tell the story of rebuilding the Temple that was planned by King David and was built by King Solomon. Esther is another story about a specific Jewish woman who saved her people by becoming a queen.

Books of Poetry

There are five books that are poems or collections of poems: Job, Psalms, Proverbs, Ecclesiastes, and Song of Songs. The words in these books don't rhyme like some poems today. But they are written in poetic language. They use beautiful word pictures and phrases to teach us about God's wisdom, strength, and love.

Books of Prophecy

The last books in the Old Testament are books by prophets or preachers. These prophets reminded the Jews to obey God. Five books were by major prophets: Isaiah, Jeremiah, Lamentations, Ezekiel, and Daniel. Their books and sermons are usually longer and they were very important to the Jewish people. There were twelve books by minor prophets: Hosea, Joel, Amos, Obadiah, Jonah, Micah, Nahum, Habakkuk, Zephaniah, Haggai, Zechariah, and Malachi. These books are usually shorter and we know less about these men. What we do know is that God gave them a special burden to help their people.

From the beginning to the end, the Old Testament reminds us that God is our creator, that we are to obey and worship him, and that he provides for our salvation through Jesus Christ.

WHAT'S IN THE NEW TESTAMENT

The New Testament part of the Bible has 27 different books. Nearly all of these books were written in the first 50 years after the death and resurrection of Jesus. Like the Old Testament, they were all written by different people in different circumstances and for different reasons. But also like the Old Testament, God's Spirit made them all come together to tell one story. They tell the story of Jesus Christ.

The books that make up the New Testament are not in order by when they are written. They are in order by what kind of book they are.

Gospels

The first four books are called Gospels: The Gospel of Matthew, Mark, Luke, and John. Each book is named for the man who wrote it. Each man told the story of Jesus, his ministry, death, and resurrection. While each writer is talking about the same person, Jesus, they each remember different stories and different parts of the same stories just like you would if you and your friend were both talking about an important person in your life. That is one thing that makes the gospels so interesting.

The Gospels are followed by another book of history called Acts, or the Acts of the Apostles. This book begins where the Gospels end—after Jesus is resurrected. It tells about the way they chose a new disciple to take Judas's place. It tells the story of the 30 years after Jesus' life on earth. It tells how the church began and how Christianity spread. Acts was written by Luke, the same man who wrote the Gospel of Luke.

What's in the New Testament

Letters

The next 21 books in the New Testament are letters or epistles. Some are letters to people. Some are letters to churches or communities. Thirteen of them were written by Paul, a famous apostle who came to know Christ after Christ's life on earth. In your Bible Paul's letters are in order by length from the longest to the shortest. There are also three letters by John (who wrote the gospel of John), two letters by Peter (a fisherman and a disciple of Jesus), one by James, and one by Jude. We don't know who the author of Hebrews was, but it was definitely someone who cared about obeying God and teaching his people.

Revelation

The last book of the New Testament is called Revelation. Revelation is an "apocalyptic" writing. That means it teaches about God's plan through word pictures and "visions" that God gave to the writer, John. This is the same John who wrote the Gospel of John.

God used a lot of people to write the books of the New Testament. He used a lot more people to bring all of those books together and to understand that they were God's message for us all. There were a lot of books written at the same time that Matthew and John and 1 Corinthians and Jude were written. The Christian leaders had to pray for wisdom that they would know which of these books had God's special stamp of approval. Those leaders talked and prayed and read and thought. They got together many times and asked themselves, "Which of these writings is God using to teach us about him? Which ones did God actually write through these writers?" As they all came to agreement they started putting books together.

A Fake New Testament

Around A.D. 150 (about 1,850 years ago) a man named Marcion tried to make his own Bible. He put together a book that he said was the whole Bible. The first thing he had done was take out the whole Old Testament! The only Gospel he had included was Luke, and Marcion himself had changed a lot of what Luke had written. Then Marcion had taken out all the letters except ten of Paul's, and he had even changed those ten letters. Marcion had changed almost everything and tried to tell people that he had put together the complete word of God.

Marcion was one of the big reasons the Christian leaders got together to pray to God and talk to each other and make a final decision about which books really belonged in the Bible. It took a long time for the official decision. (The official announcement was made in A.D. 393, about 1,600 years ago.) But even before that God had shown the church leaders that the 27 books we know as the New Testament were the books that Christians kept reading and reading and learning from. That was an exciting discovery!

The New Testament teaches us how Christ lived and how we should live. It tells us about the sticky situations churches can get into and how the church needs to get along. The New Testament gives us hope that Jesus is coming again some day and we will have a home with him in heaven.

WHO'S WHO

Do you know who the MVPs (most valuable persons) in the Bible are? This section tells you. They are listed in order of when they were born.

(For something about Jesus, look in "Life and Ministry of Jesus.")

Adam and Eve

the very beginning

Adam and Eve are the parents of the human race. God created them to live in the Garden of Eden and to be his friends.

Satan said God was not being good to Eve and Adam. Eve believed Satan. She disobeyed God and convinced Adam to join her in disobeying.

Because they sinned, God sent them from the garden. Sickness and death entered the world. But God promised a Savior.

(Genesis 1:26–5:5)

Noah

some time before 2500 B.C.

Noah and his family were the only people God saved from the worldwide flood.

Noah was a righteous man who loved the Lord. He was the only person who listened to God. Everyone else ignored God.

God told Noah to build a huge boat and fill it with food for his family and for the animals he would send. Noah and his family followed God's instructions.

(Genesis 5:29–10:32)

Job

around 2200 B.C.

Job is known for his patience. God allowed Satan to take away all of Job's wealth, family, and finally health. Satan said Job served God only because he had an easy life.

But God knew that Job loved him, not just the things God gave him. Job did not know why he was having so much trouble. Job's friends said he did something wrong.

In the end Job knew God was even more powerful than he thought. God gave back Job's wealth and gave him a new family, too. *(Job 1–42)*

Abraham and Sarah

(2166 B.C.)

Abraham and Sarah were the father and mother of God's people, the Jews.

God promised Abraham he would have more children than the stars in the sky. Abraham and Sarah were old and still had no children. Finally, when Abraham was 100 years old and Sarah was 90, God gave them a son named Isaac.

God tested Abraham's faith many times. But Abraham trusted God, and that made him an example to us all. *(Genesis 11-25)*

Isaac and Rebekah

2066 B.C.

Isaac was the son of Abraham and Sarah—the son that God had promised them.

Isaac married Rebekah. At first they couldn't have a baby, just like Abraham and Sarah. But Isaac prayed, and God gave them twin sons. God told Rebekah that the younger one would rule over the older one.

Rebekah did not wait for God to fulfill his promise. Instead, she told Jacob, the younger, to trick his father, Isaac, so he would get the family leadership.

Jacob had to run away from Esau, his angry brother.
(Genesis 17:15–35:29)

Jacob and Rachel

2006 B.C.

Jacob was the unlikely heir of God's promise to make a nation from Abraham and Sarah.

Jacob the tricker was tricked by his uncle Laban. Laban tricked Jacob into marrying Leah. Jacob had to work many years in order to marry Rachel, the one he really loved.

Rachel did not have children at first. She was jealous of her sister Leah who did have children. Rachel was afraid Jacob did not love her. Finally God gave Rachel two sons, Joseph and Benjamin. Rachel died soon after that.

Jacob learned to trust God and stop tricking people. Then God changed his name to Israel. His sons and two grandsons became the twelve tribes of Israel.
(Genesis 25–50)

Joseph

1915 B.C.

Joseph was Jacob's favorite son. Joseph loved God and lived a pure life. But that didn't save him from trouble.

Joseph's jealous brothers plotted to kill him but sold him into slavery. He became the trusted slave of an Egyptian leader. Later, he was accused of crimes, put in prison, and forgotten.

Finally, Joseph was called to tell the meaning of a dream Pharaoh had. Overnight, Joseph became second to Pharaoh in all of Egypt!

Because of famine, Joseph's brothers went to Egypt to buy food. They did not recognize their brother. He tested them. When he knew they were sorry for their sin, he let them know he was Joseph. What a reunion there was!

(Genesis 30–50)

Moses

1526 B.C.

Moses was a Hebrew who grew up in Egypt, escaped to the desert, and returned to free God's people from slavery.

The Egyptians did not want to lose their slaves. But after God sent 10 plagues, the Egyptians finally let them go.

Moses had a hard time leading the stubborn people. They often did not want to obey God. The short trip to the Promised Land became a 40-year journey. Moses was a kind, strong leader who loved God and God's people.

(Exodus, Leviticus, Numbers, and Deuteronomy)

Joshua

around 1500 B.C.

Joshua was a faithful helper to Moses. God chose him to take Moses' place when he died. He was one of the 12 spies who went into the Promised Land. Only he and Caleb trusted God to give them victory.

Joshua actually led the people into the Promised Land. He also led the battle of Jericho.

Joshua's well known words are, "Choose today whom you will serve . . . But as for me and my family, we will serve the Lord" (Joshua 24:15).

(Exodus 17:9-14; Joshua 1–24)

Ruth

between 1375 and 1050 B.C.

Ruth is one of two women who have books in the Bible named for them. Ruth was not an Israelite; she was from the land of Moab. Her people worshiped idols, not the true God.

But Ruth married an Israelite man in Moab. He and his brothers and father died. Naomi, Ruth's mother-in-law, was returning to Bethlehem. Ruth chose to go with Naomi and follow the Lord.

Ruth took care of her mother-in-law. Then God gave Ruth a new husband who loved the Lord too. God gave Ruth and Boaz a son named Obed. He became the grandfather of King David.

(Ruth 1–4)

Hannah

around 1150 B.C.

Hannah was a godly wife who longed to be a mother. She prayed very hard and asked God for a son. Hannah made a strange promise to God. She said she would give her son back to the Lord.

God said yes to Hannah and gave her a son. Hannah praised God and thanked him for his kindness to her. She named her son

Samuel. Hannah loved Samuel deeply. But she kept her promise. When Samuel was about three years old, Hannah took him to live with the High Priest Eli.

(1 Samuel 1–2)

Samuel

1105 B.C.

Samuel was a prophet and priest for the people of Israel. Before he was born, his mother asked God for a son. She dedicated him to serve the Lord.

From the time he was a little tot, Samuel lived with Eli, the High Priest. Samuel learned to listen to the Lord's voice. He obeyed him and became a great spiritual leader for his people.

Samuel was the priest who anointed Saul as king, and later David, too.

(1 Samuel 1–28)

Saul

1080 B.C.

Saul was the first king of Israel. At first he was humble and obeyed God. He asked the prophet Samuel to help him. But later he disobeyed God and Samuel said the Lord would give the kingdom to someone else.

Saul continued to reign for 40 years. During much of that time he chased David and tried to kill him. David waited patiently for God to give him the kingdom. Saul and his sons were killed the same day in a battle with the Philistines.

(1 Samuel 9–31)

Who's Who

David

1050 B.C.

David was the best known king of Israel. He became king after Saul was killed. The people loved David. That made Saul jealous. For many years before he became king, David had to run away from Saul.

David was an excellent soldier. He learned his fighting skills from his years as a shepherd, fighting off lions and bears. That's how he killed the powerful giant Goliath.

David was also a musician and poet. He played the harp and wrote many of the psalms. People use his prayers and praise songs to worship God today.

David loved God, but he still sinned. He always was truly sorry and asked God to forgive him.

God called David "a man after my own heart" (Acts 13:22).
(1 Samuel 16–31; 2 Samuel 1–24; 1 Kings 1–2)

Solomon

around 1000 B.C.

Solomon is known as the wisest man who ever lived. Solomon was the son of King David and Bathsheba. He was the third king of Israel.

God allowed Solomon to build the Temple in Jerusalem where the Jewish people worshiped God. It was famous for its beauty.

Solomon wrote many proverbs, some psalms, Ecclesiastes, and the Song of Songs in the Old Testament.

In spite of his wisdom, Solomon disobeyed God in a very important matter. He married many wives from foreign countries who worshiped idols. The Lord divided Solomon's kingdom after he died.
(2 Samuel 12:24–24:25; 1 Kings 1:1–11:43)

Elijah

around 900 B.C.

Elijah was a prophet so close to God that he never died; God took him straight to heaven!

God let Elijah do many important miracles. Elijah declared there would be no rain till he said so. Famine resulted. God used Elijah to bring a dead boy back to life.

Elijah took a bold stand against the prophets of Baal. King Ahab and Queen Jezebel were supporting Baal worship. Elijah challenged all the prophets of Baal to prove who was the real God. Nothing happened when the priests of Baal prayed to their god. When Elijah prayed to the Lord, God answered immediately!

(1 Kings 17:1–22:53; 2 Kings 1:1–2:11)

Jonah

around 800 B.C.

Jonah was the prophet who tried to run away from God. He did not want to tell the wicked people of Nineveh to turn to God because he knew God would forgive them if they did. It took a storm at sea and rescue by a huge fish for Jonah to change his mind. He finally did what he was supposed to. But he never got over the fact that the people listened and were forgiven.

(Jonah 1–4)

Isaiah

around 750 B.C.

Isaiah was an Israelite who became a prophet when he saw the Lord in heaven. It made him very aware of his sinfulness to see God in all his holiness. But God forgave him and Isaiah was never the same after that. He faithfully preached about God's judgment and hope. Many of his prophecies are about the Messiah.

(Isaiah 1–66)

Jeremiah

around 650 B.C.

Jeremiah is often called the weeping prophet. He warned his people about coming judgment but they would not listen to him. They accused him of being a traitor. He was mocked and abused for telling God's message, but he did not give up. Jeremiah was taken away into captivity along with the people from Jerusalem. He is called the weeping prophet because no one ever listened to him and all the bad things happened that God said would happen.

(Jeremiah 1–52; Lamentations 1–5)

Daniel

around 625 B.C.

Daniel was a young Jewish man who became an adviser to four Babylonian kings while an exile in Babylonia. He worshiped God faithfully in Babylon even when his life was on the line. Once he was put into a den of hungry lions because he prayed to the Lord. But God protected him and kept him alive.

God gave Daniel the ability to tell the meaning of dreams. He also prophesied about the end times.

(Daniel 1–12)

Ezra

around 500 B.C.

Ezra was a faithful Jewish priest while a captive in Persia. King Artaxerxes allowed him to take other captives back to Jerusalem. They took things they needed to worship the Lord.

Ezra studied God's law and taught the people so they could repent and turn back to God.

(Ezra 1–10)

Esther

around 500 B.C.

Esther is the second woman with a book of the Bible named after her. Esther was a young Jewish woman whom God used to save her people from all being killed. She became queen to King Xerxes. A palace official plotted to kill all the Jews in Persia. Queen Esther was able to expose the plan and save the Jews.

The Jewish holiday Purim is still celebrated in memory of that victory.

(Esther 1–10)

NOTE: All the people of New Testament times lived during the first century A.D., between 0 and 100.

Barnabas

Barnabas was a Christian leader in the early church. His name means "son of encouragement." The apostles called him that because he was always helping people. He sold a piece of property and gave the money to help the needy.

Barnabas traveled with Paul, taking the gospel to people who had not heard about Jesus.

(Acts 4:36-37; 9:27–15:39)

Who's Who

Nicodemus

Nicodemus was a Jewish religious leader who went to talk with Jesus at night. He asked Jesus many questions but did not really understand at first. Later on, he tried to stand up for Jesus in the religious meetings. The other leaders made fun of him. After Jesus was crucified, Nicodemus helped Joseph of Arimathea bury Jesus. By then he understood that Jesus is God's Son.

(John 3:1-21; 7:50-52; 19:39-40)

Aquila and Priscilla

Aquila and Priscilla were a husband and wife team who worked and traveled with Paul. They were Jewish Christians from Rome who helped others understand the gospel. They opened their home as a church and made their living making tents.

(Acts 18; Romans 16:3-5; 1 Corinthians 16:19)

Paul

Paul was a missionary, preacher, and writer of Scripture. God changed him from a man who hated Jesus and his followers to one of Jesus' most devoted followers. He took three missionary journeys to take the gospel to places all over the Roman empire.

People did not always like what he had to say. Paul was beaten, stoned, imprisoned, and harassed many times because of his love for Christ.

Paul wrote 13 of the New Testament books: Romans, 1 Corinthians, 2 Corinthians, Galatians, Ephesians, Colossians, 1 Thessalonians, 2 Thessalonians, 1 Timothy, 2 Timothy, Titus, Philemon.

(Acts 7:58–28:31 and the letters he wrote.)

Timothy

Timothy was like a son to the apostle Paul. He traveled on missionary journeys with him. Paul also sent Timothy to help churches solve problems. To some of these churches he served as pastor.

Paul wrote two letters to Timothy, encouraging and instructing him in his duties as a pastor. Timothy may have been with Paul when he died.

(Acts 16:1-5; Romans 16:21; Philippians 1:1)

KEY EVENTS

Abraham Leaves Ur

1. Ur
Ur of the Chaldeans was a thriving city with businesses and a large library. Abraham was probably well educated. When the Lord called him to leave Ur, he had to leave all the comforts of home. *(Genesis 11:27-32)*

2. Haran
Abraham, his father Terah, wife Sarah, and nephew Lot set out from Ur. They followed the Tigris and Euphrates rivers instead of crossing the desert. They stopped in Haran. After Terah died, Abraham continued his journey. *(Genesis 12:1-5)*

3. Canaan
From Haran, Abraham and his family traveled to Shechem. God told Abraham he would give Canaan to Abraham's children *(Genesis 12:6-7)*. Abraham built an altar to the Lord between Bethel and Ai, then continued to the Negeb.

4. Egypt, Bethel
Because of a famine in Canaan, Abraham went to Egypt. Afterward, he returned to Bethel with his wife and nephew. He had become very wealthy. He prayed to the Lord again. *(Genesis 12:10–13:18)*

Jacob Settles in Canaan

1. Beersheba
Jacob grew up in Beersheba, but ran away from home after

tricking his father, Isaac, and making Esau furious. *(Genesis 27:42-45)*

2. Bethel

He stopped in Bethel where he had a dream of angels going up and down a ladder or staircase to heaven. God promised him Canaan for his descendants. *(Genesis 28:10-22)*

3. Haran

In Haran, Laban tricked Jacob. Jacob worked 7 years before he was allowed to have Rachel as his wife. After 20 years of hard work and mistreatment, Jacob decided to return to Canaan. *(Genesis 31:36-42)*

4. Canaan

Jacob was afraid of Esau, and sent gifts to him. During the night, God wrestled with Jacob. God changed Jacob's name to Israel *(Genesis 32:22-31)*. Jacob traveled to Shechem where he bought a piece of property and set up an altar to worship the Lord *(Genesis 33:18-20)*.

The Exodus

1. Marah, Elim, Rephidim

Moses crossed the Red Sea, then led the people south. The desert was hot and dry, but God provided water and food. *(Exodus 14:22-25; 16:1, 13-15)*

2. Mount Sinai

God appeared to Moses on this mountain. Then he sent him to lead Israel out of Egypt *(Exodus 3:1-2)*. Moses returned with the people. For almost a year, they camped at the foot of Mount Sinai. God gave them the Ten Commandments and the plan for the Tabernacle *(Exodus 19-40)*.

3. Kadesh-barnea

Spies went into the Promised Land but 10 of the 12 gave a negative report. The people were scared and would not obey God's command to go in. God made that entire generation wander for 38 years in the desert. *(Numbers 14)*

4. Jericho

God waited till all the adults who had refused to enter the Promised Land the first time had died. Then he let the Israelites enter the land. Moses did not get to go; he died on Mount Nebo. Joshua led the people across the Jordan River on dry land, defeated Jericho, and began to take Canaan. *(Joshua 1-6)*

Conquest of Canaan

1. Jordan River

The priests carried the Ark of the Covenant into the Jordan River. The water stopped and everyone crossed over on dry ground *(Joshua 2:1-4:24)*. Once in the Promised Land, they camped at Gilgal and celebrated Passover. An angel appeared to Joshua *(Joshua 5:1-15)*.

2. Jericho, Ai

Joshua and the people obeyed God and broke the walls of Jericho down by marching around the city *(Joshua 6:1-27)*. But because of Achan's sin, the Israelites were unable to take the next city, Ai. After dealing with Achan's disobedience, they captured Ai *(Joshua 7:1-8:29)*.

3. Mount Ebal, Mount Gerizim

Joshua, the priests, and the people renewed their covenant with God. *(Joshua 8:30-35)*

4. Valley of Aijalon

Five kings attacked the city of Gibeon, which had made a treaty with the Israelites. Joshua and his troops joined the battle. It lasted all day, and Joshua asked God to make the sun stand still until the Israelites defeated the enemy. *(Joshua 10:1-43)*

5. Hazor

Another group of kings joined together to fight Israel. But God gave his people the victory. *(Joshua 11:1-23)*

6. Shiloh

Many of the enemy armies were defeated and the Israelites enjoyed a time of peace. They gathered in Shiloh and set up the Tabernacle to worship the Lord. *(Joshua 18:1-19:51)*

Formation of the Kingdom

1. Ramah

Saul was looking for his father's lost donkeys. He did not know that the prophet Samuel was waiting for him at Ramah. The people wanted a king, and God told Samuel to anoint Saul as king of Israel. The modest Saul was surprised by Samuel's words and actions. *(1 Samuel 10:1)*

2. Jabesh Gilead

The people of Jabesh Gilead asked Saul for help against their enemies, the Ammonites. Saul gathered an army at Bezek and they rescued the town of Jabesh. The people were happy to see God's blessing on their hero. They celebrated by going to Gilgal to worship God and confirm Saul as their new king. *(1 Samuel 11:1-15)*

3. Elah

Saul was king but he allowed the giant Goliath to mock God's people. David accepted Goliath's challenge to fight one-on-one.

Key Events ▬▬▬▬▬▬▬

David killed the Philistine in the valley of Elah with his shepherd's sling and a stone. Then the Israelites chased the Philistines to their towns of Gath and Ekron and defeated them. After that, David became very popular. *(1 Samuel 17:1-58)*

4. Hebron

King Saul was jealous of David because the people loved him. For years, Saul chased David and tried to kill him. David never hurt Saul, though he had many opportunities to kill him. David waited for God's timing. Then Saul was killed in battle by the Philistines. The people of Hebron made David king of Judah. *(2 Samuel 2:4)*

5. Jerusalem

Seven and a half years after Saul's death, David became king over all the tribes of Israel and made Jerusalem his capital. *(2 Samuel 5:4-5)*

The Exile

1. Judah

Through most of Judah's history, God's people turned their backs on the Lord. God warned the people many times to turn back to him. A few kings even tried to reform the people. But the changes never lasted. *(Isaiah 6:8-13)*

2. Babylonia

Finally God sent King Nebuchadnezzer to take the people of Judah captive. He destroyed Jerusalem and took the people to Babylonia. The prophet Ezekiel brought God's messages to them while they were there. They stayed for 70 years before being allowed to return. *(2 Chronicles 36:15-21)*

3. Jerusalem

After many years, God moved the heart of Cyrus to allow some of the exiles to return to Jerusalem to repair the Temple. Zerubbabel led the first group of exiles back *(Ezra 1:1-8)*. Years later, Ezra led another group of exiles on the dangerous journey *(Ezra 7:1-10)*. Esther and some others stayed behind *(Esther 1–10)*.

Jesus' Travels

1. Bethlehem, Nazareth

Jesus was born in Bethlehem. His parents took him to the Temple in Jerusalem to dedicate him as required by the law. Later they fled to Egypt to escape King Herod's wrath. When it was safe, they returned to Nazareth, where Jesus grew up. At age 12 he went with his family to Jerusalem for Passover and spoke with the religious leaders. *(Luke 2)*

2. Jordan River

Jesus was baptized in the Jordan River by his cousin John the Baptist. Then the Holy Spirit led Jesus to the desert where Satan tempted him for 40 days. Jesus answered the Devil with Scripture and resisted his temptations. Then Jesus was ready for ministry. *(Matthew 3:13-17; Luke 4:1-13)*

3. Capernaum

Jesus spent the last three years of his life showing people the Kingdom of God. He made his headquarters in Capernaum and traveled throughout Israel preaching, teaching, and healing the sick *(Matthew 9:35)*. He called several of his disciples from their fishing nets on the Sea of Galilee.

Near Capernaum, Jesus gave his Sermon on the Mount,

including the Beatitudes. *(Matthew 5–7)*

4. Nazareth
In his hometown of Nazareth, Jesus did not do many miracles because his neighbors did not believe in him. *(Matthew 13:53-58)*

5. Sea of Galilee
By the Sea of Galilee, Jesus fed 5,000 men plus women and children with just five loaves of bread and two fish. *(Matthew 14:13-21)*

6. Tyre
In Tyre, a Gentile woman asked Jesus for mercy and healing for her daughter. Jesus was amazed at her faith and granted her request. *(Matthew 15:21-28)*

7. Caesarea Philippi
It was at Caesarea Philippi that Jesus' disciple Peter first acknowledged that Jesus is the Christ, the Son of God. *(Matthew 16:13-20)*

8. Jericho
The tax collector Zacchaeus lived in Jericho and Jesus went to his house to take him salvation. *(Luke 19:1-10)*

9. Bethany
In Bethany Jesus brought his good friend Lazarus back to life. *(John 11:1-44)*

10. Jerusalem
Jerusalem was the site of many discussions with the Pharisees and the common people. It was there Jesus gave his life for the sin of the world, then was buried and raised back to life. *(John 18–21)*

Paul's First Missionary Journey
Summary: Paul, Barnabas, and John Mark were sent by the

church in Antioch to go to west. After awhile, John Mark left them and it was a long time before Paul trusted him again. Paul always took his message to the Jews first. But usually they did not want to hear about Jesus. Then Paul would speak to the Gentiles who usually were eager to hear the Good News of life in Christ. That made the Jews jealous and angry. Paul's life was often in danger. With so many Gentiles becoming believers, the church had to decide if they first had to become Jews. Paul spoke clearly that faith is what makes anyone a Christian—not keeping the law. (Acts 13–14)

Paul's Second Missionary Journey

Summary: Barnabas wanted to take John Mark again but Paul did not want to. They disagreed and decided to go separate ways. Paul took Silas with him to visit the believers in the towns he had visited on his first trip. Paul met many people who became his lifelong fellow believers and friends. Best known are Timothy, Lydia, Priscilla, and Aquila. Paul had a vision of a man in Macedonia asking him to help him. It was on this trip that Paul and Silas were unfairly put in jail and God sent an earthquake to break them out. As a result, the jailer and his family became Christians. (Acts 15:36–18:22)

Paul's Third Missionary Journey

Summary: Paul returned a third time to the cities he had visited before. Many of his New Testament letters are to the churches in those cities. His third trip was to clear up any misunderstandings that the believers had. (Acts 18:23–20:38)

Paul found some people who had only heard John the Baptist's message. They did not know that Jesus had already come. So Paul gave them the complete facts and they became believers and received the Holy Spirit. Others who had been involved in the occult burned their sorcery scrolls. It amounted to a great deal of money. However some men who were silversmiths and made idols of the goddess Artemis did not want to lose their jobs. They caused a riot to get Paul to stop talking about the true God. On this last trip, Paul made sure to clear up any misunderstandings that the believers had. He also said his last farewell to the elders of the Ephesian church before he returned to Jerusalem to report what God had done among the Gentiles. *(Acts 21:17-19)*

Paul then returned to Jerusalem to report what God had done. *(Acts 21:17-19)*